Contributions to Management Science

The series *Contributions to Management Science* contains research publications in all fields of business and management science. These publications are primarily monographs and multiple author works containing new research results, and also feature selected conference-based publications are also considered. The focus of the series lies in presenting the development of latest theoretical and empirical research across different viewpoints.

This book series is indexed in Scopus.

More information about this series at https://link.springer.com/bookseries/1505

Mojca Ramšak

Social Impact of Wine Marketing

The Challenge of Digital Technologies to Regulation

Springer

Mojca Ramšak
Faculty of Arts and Faculty of Medicine
University of Ljubljana
Ljubljana, Slovenia

ISSN 1431-1941 ISSN 2197-716X (electronic)
Contributions to Management Science
ISBN 978-3-030-89223-4 ISBN 978-3-030-89224-1 (eBook)
https://doi.org/10.1007/978-3-030-89224-1

This Springer imprint is published by the registered company Springer Nature Switzerland AG.
The registered company address is: Gewerbestrasse 11, 6330 Cham, Switzerland

Acknowledgments

I was not expected to get into digital and alcohol, but I was encouraged to do so after a series of events shifted my focus and priorities. I changed my mind due to two factors. First, the hopelessness of living with an alcoholic hit me hard when a close friend took her own life due to family alcohol problems. Second, parental helplessness haunted me after my son and his high school classmates were introduced to the "wet culture." This was one of the reasons I began following outside drinking encouragements, and I was frankly astounded, no matter how much I had previously written about alcohol, at how the alcohol industry seduces young people to drink with impunity. Unfortunately, some young people have been unable to escape the alcohol industry's tricks and have become enslaved by binge drinking or, worse, permanently addicted.

That is why I wrote this book for all those who have tried to drown their sorrows by drinking excessively, for those who have lost themselves or someone close to them as a result of excessive drinking, and for those who could not bear living with an alcoholic and preferred to leave this world.

Contents

List of Figures

Chapter 1
Introduction: Wine and Technology Between Cultural Attitudes to Alcohol, Sales, Legislation, and Health

I always think the opening moments of a party are the hardest, before everyone has had enough to drink.

Stephanie Clifford, Everybody Rise

Abstract The introduction explains the book's goals as well as a broad red threat. It describes the scope and circumstances of digitalization in the wine industry, which has spread to include wine production and marketing through the use of modern technologies and robotics. Because drinking culture, alcohol regulation, and alcohol preventative and curative health initiatives are all linked and complex, it emphasizes alcohol consumption patterns and their relationship to culture. The introduction also explains why the book relies on so many various sources and how they are combined to provide a comprehensive picture of wine marketing's social impact, along with the challenges of digital technology and legal regulation.

This monograph *Social Impact of Wine Marketing—The Challenge of Digital Technologies to Regulation* presents the social and cultural ideas and evidence in the field of wine e-marketing, increased alcohol consumption, and legal regulation, drawing on a wide range of sources. The aim of this book is to decode the strategies of alcohol advertising, which are cleverly embedded in the contexts of hedonism, luxury, social power and influence, and the concept of choice. The alcohol industry, whose advertising tactics are always one step ahead of legal regulation and public health, relies heavily on the development of new technologies. Their use is ubiquitous and usually takes place under the radar of legal regulation. The fil rouge of the idea for the topic selection is the ingenuity of the alcohol industry to market their excess alcohol and create lifelong consumers. The pandemics COVID-19 in 2020 and 2021 further accelerated the use of remote drinking and socialization technologies, and alcohol consumption increased significantly. As public health worldwide was predominantly concerned with combating infectious diseases and many other

M. Ramšak, *Social Impact of Wine Marketing*, Contributions to Management Science, https://doi.org/10.1007/978-3-030-89224-1_1

prevention programs were discontinued or cut, the alcohol industry also targeted that segment of the population that had previously only drank occasionally or not at all.

This book looks at how digital alcohol marketing is used, as well as the social and cultural elements that have influenced its success. What is the true goal of digital development in the alcohol industry? Even if we are completely oblivious to all forms of alcohol advertising, the answer is obvious. The alcohol industry invests in digital advertising in order to sell alcohol to those who are not yet addicted and do not have culturally specific drinking habits. The insidious ways in which alcohol is marketed to different target groups, such as women and men, youth, families, are precisely described through accurate explanations and cases from the global environment. The way the alcohol industry circumvents legislation, or the ineffectiveness of self-regulation, has negative consequences that can no longer be prevented by public health programs, although they too are moving with the times and using modern technology to reduce, prevent, and control alcohol consumption. The intentions of the alcohol industry are difficult to prove, especially without a broader humanistic understanding of alcohol consumption over time and across cultures. Therefore, the drinking practices and attitudes toward alcohol imposed directly or subtly by the alcohol industry through advertising are also subject to anthropological commentary.

Recently, the term "digiwine" has been introduced. It can be understood in two contexts; one refers to the production, the other to the sale of wine. In this book, however, the focus is on the second meaning of the term.

The term "digiwine" as a neologism refers to the production and/or marketing of wine through the use of new technologies and robotics (e.g., vineyard information systems, sensor units, weather stations, drones, digital maps, mobile robots for weeding and harvesting in the vineyard; autonomous robots using a special band of ultraviolet light, UV-C, to treat the vines and prevent mildew). Great changes have taken place in wine production. Today, vineyards in many places are robotized and digitized. All vineyard data can be optimized through the Vineyard Information System (eVineyard). The system provides records, insights into the cost of certain operations, calculates, and schedules time spent in the vineyard by connecting to a nearby weather station and sensor units in the vineyard that pull in and send weather data, warn of hazards, trigger irrigation systems when needed, and help decide when to spray for powdery mildew and botrytis. The system has crop tracking and GPS functions for tractors and takes into account vineyard characteristics. Modernized winemakers use technologies such as drones that monitor vine growth and health from the air and show changes on digital maps. Self-charging soil sensors, or those installed between wire supports in a vineyard, send information about soil, temperature, moisture, grapes, leaves, and vines to a computer. Mobile robots wander between rows in the vineyard, collecting various data and performing simple "manual" tasks such as weeding and picking grapes. All these measuring and working processes enable better fertility of the vines and a higher wine production. However, since at least the Industrial Revolution, the dilemma of whether or not to use advanced technology instead of a human hand has been a challenging one. The main dilemma is whether we are replacing people and depriving them of their right to work and earn a living. When a company wishes to use real people but the pool of local workers is not available due to the migration from rural areas, robots may be the only option. Even though winemakers do not want their wineries to become completely automated, it is the only choice if workers in the cellars or vineyards are no longer accessible or willing to work. Due to labor scarcity, winemakers are considering self-automating the production process.

The word "digiwine" is also used in the alcohol sector to indicate digital strategies and internet solutions for more effective wine sales (e.g., wearable technology, digital labels, wine apps for smartphones, online wine tastings, online drinking games, social media, blogs, and videos). Artificial intelligence and new technologies in grape production and wine marketing are influencing wine consumption. Globally, wine production is greater than consumption. In 2020, global wine consumption was slightly down, with COVID-19 triggering a decline. After a sharp decline in consumption in the first half of 2020, there was some recovery in the second half. Higher-end wines and sparkling wines were the most affected, due to the closure of restaurants and the cancelation of many events. Considering that about 40 million hectoliters of wine go unused every year, digital marketing is expected to intensify. The main principle of alcohol marketing is to disguise its advertising as consumer entertainment and hedonism. The purpose of this marketing is to loosen the boundary between advertising and entertainment, which allows marketers to disguise and circumvent the harmful effects of alcohol and alcohol advertisers' codes of ethics and increase wine consumption.

The wine industry is on the hunt for new customers, particularly among the young. Improvements from "smart vineyards" that allow for larger and higher quality harvests to aggressive Internet marketing aim to reach everyone, starting with the youngest at kindergarten age. Young people as potential and end consumers are a huge niche market because they are exposed at an early age to the virtual environment they are connected to, primarily through smartphones, which distracts them from real life and what should be more important to them. As a result, they also have a fairly low level of self-reflection and critical thinking and passively engage with the online offering, which wine marketing uses to its advantage to persuade them to drink. As young people are only at the stage of shaping their lives, terms such as "cultural drinker," "social drinker," and "wine connoisseur" are easily inculcated in them, as a natural consequence of the so-called "wet cultures" with high availability of alcohol, tolerance of the negative consequences of consumption and lack of protective measures. To some extent, legislation protects against harmful advertising and alcohol consumption, but the wine and alcohol industry in general, well versed in digital marketing trends, has invented many attractive digital forms of marketing that are not covered by the law. They encourage young people to drink so that they eventually become lifelong drinkers and alcohol consumption becomes a natural part of their lifestyle. Digital alcohol marketing almost completely ignores the legal place and time of alcohol sales and the age of the consumer and introduces many covert forms of advertising.

Most alcohol marketing today is interactive, hybrid and simultaneous, and takes place in parallel through social media, with videos on the Internet, apps on mobile applications, and in traditional ways through ads in the media, on billboards. Digital alcohol marketing is a sophisticated guerrilla method that largely and easily circumvents national alcohol advertising laws, as the targeted, predominantly (too) young population spontaneously passes on free, popular games and other likeable marketing messages to their friends, as no one checks whether alcohol marketing really excludes minors. In addition to alcohol addiction, the alcohol industry, through games, alcohol applications, and examples from the world of media stars, also arouses an uncontrolled need for mobile phones and similar devices, causing a double addiction.

In order to compare the characteristics of alcohol advertising in the digital world and to some extent in the analog world, the actual drinking culture, alcohol legislation, and health programs, a systematic research monitoring of the situation was carried out. Drawing on historical, anthropological, and other sources from earlier eras, the book interweaves data with social and historical explanations of some of the most common forms of drinking and advertising culture. Multiple sources were used and examined, such as: Alcohol marketing trends, strategies and tools from marketing literature, wine and marketing magazines; global and national statistics on alcohol consumption and its consequences; national marketing and alcohol laws and alcohol industry self-regulatory documents; cases of inappropriate alcohol advertising complained to advertising tribunals; policies in the area of prevention of excessive alcohol consumption; monitoring of governmental and nongovernmental organizations that track alcohol advertising at the regional or global level; systematically collected and analytically annotated forms of alcohol advertising by the wine industry, small winemakers and wholesalers on social networks, in classic publications (catalogs, billboards, media ads), promotion and branding with special discounts for target groups, various alcohol apps for smartphones, drinking games, prize games, etc. Empirically verifiable forms of social normalization of alcohol consumption through indirect advertising (e.g., advertising using public figures, advertising in film and the arts, advertising to children and families) and health programs have been examined. The overlap of this information reveals the astonishing arrogance of the alcohol industry. It deliberately flies under the radar of legislation, policy makers, and public health and will continue to do so with well-thought-out advertising strategies. In doing so, it also reveals the helplessness of society and public health campaigns to prevent excessive alcohol consumption.

The anthropological study of alcohol differs in its focus from the epidemiological, wrote Dwight Heath, who published extensively on the topic of alcohol consumption patterns and their relationship to culture (Heath, 2010). We can summarize his idea of the distinction between the anthropological and epidemiological perspectives on alcohol consumption, which makes him one of the main critics of the new alcohol prohibitions, as follows: Anthropology tends to focus on beliefs and behaviors, giving at least equal attention to "normal" and "deviant" patterns related to alcohol use, with an emphasis on social and legal norms, attitudes, values, and socialization; whereas epidemiology tends to focus on "alcoholism" defined in different ways, implying that habitual drinking is inevitably associated with some kinds of problems, and consequently the prevention of alcoholism, or at least the manipulation of drinking practices (Heath, 2010: 41, 42). Despite the time lag in formulating his thoughts, I myself hold a similar conviction, namely that without a culturally specific insight into the reasons for alcohol consumption and intoxication, this area cannot be adequately regulated either legally or medically.

In the introductory words of the British social anthropologist Mary Douglas, known for her writings on human culture and symbolism, and the above-mentioned American anthropologist Dwight Heath, two of the world's leading anthropological authorities on alcohol, written for the volume *Constructive Drinking: Perspectives on Drink from Anthropology* (first published in 1987, reprinted in 2003 and 2010), we read that even in anthropology alcohol consumption is sometimes viewed from a problem or medical angle. But fundamentally, most research focuses on drinking as a form of ritual, a social act performed in an accepted social context, because in most cultures alcohol is a normal accompaniment to a celebration. Where alcohol is an important food, patterns of sharing can help to understand social organization. Symbolic, religious, and other beliefs associated with such drinks are often important. There are plausible links to the symbolic nature of alcohol, for example, in toasting, the obligation to accept an offered drink, and other widespread and emotionally charged customs. Drinks also function as markers of personal identity and the boundaries of inclusion and exclusion. In general, status inconsistency appears to be a good predictor of increased alcohol consumption in both sexes. In this case, alcohol is a depressant that relieves anxiety, anomie, and tension stemming from a variety of sources. In small doses, alcohol is also considered an aphrodisiac, although in large quantities it is clearly a depressant drug. In many societies, it is also associated with leisure and other forms of recreation. If we focus on alcohol abuse, the work of anthropologists suggests that the most effective way to control it is through socialization. Community authority, community rituals, community solidarity seem to bring drinking under control. But sometimes the form of community is aggressively competitive, and the drinker who follows its customs puts his health at risk (Douglas, 2010: 4, 6, 8; Heath, 2010: 30, 31, 34, 39, 40).

Dwight Heath (2010) classified the anthropological research on alcohol and summarized the main generalizations that emerge from the cross-cultural study of alcohol research in several focal points:

- In most societies, drinking is essentially a social act and, as such, is embedded in a context of values, attitudes, and other norms.
- These values, attitudes, and norms represent important sociocultural factors that influence the effects of drinking, regardless of how important biochemical, physiological, and pharmacokinetic factors may be in this context.
- The consumption of alcoholic beverages is usually associated with rules about who can and cannot drink how much of what, in what context, in the company of whom, and so on. Often such rules are associated with particularly strong emotions and sanctions.
- The value of alcohol in promoting relaxation and sociability is emphasized in many populations.

- When alcohol-related problems do occur, they are clearly related to the modalities of alcohol consumption and usually to values, attitudes, and norms about drinking.
- Attempts to ban alcohol have never been successful unless formulated in the form of sacred or supernatural rules (Heath, 2010: 46).

Following these ground rules for alcohol's role in society, this book explains the marketing efforts of the alcohol industry, which advertises so successfully because it has internalized the anthropological rules of drinking. Because of the lack of awareness of the interconnections of the anthropological rules of drinking, legal regulation, and health prevention fall by the wayside.

References

Douglas, M. (2010). A distinctive anthropological perspective. In *Constructive drinking. Perspectives on drink from anthropology. Mary Douglas collected works, volume X* (pp. 3–15). Routledge.

Heath, D. (2010). A decade of development in the anthropological study of alcohol use, 1970–1980. In *Constructive drinking. Perspectives on drink from anthropology. Mary Douglas collected works, volume X* (pp. 16–69). Routledge.

Chapter 2
The Greatest Tricks of Digital Alcohol Marketing: The Consumer's Voice and Alcohol e-Marketing

I think that it is a great tragedy that a child can lose their mother, father, sister or brother, because you and I made a decision that getting loaded was more important than they are.

Pamela Barrett, Tales of the Titmouse

Abstract In this chapter, the importance of consumer voice from the pre-industrial era to hyperinformation in the Internet age is discussed. The historical evolution of consumer voice is important in understanding the seeming cacophony of voices emanating from the alcohol industry or its marketing practices, particularly when attempting to disguise or distort the harmful effects of alcohol. It then explains the paradigms such as engagement, targeted advertising, and a comprehensive 360-degree strategy that the alcohol industry uses to try to reach consumers across the media landscape. The goal is to create an environment in which consumers interact with the brand and become acquainted with the product. Alcohol companies work with digital marketing experts to develop marketing-connected environments that promote products.

The evolution of the consumer's voice went through several phases, and as one scholar of marketing and consumer behavior Umit Kucuk notes, and the industrial revolution was to manufacturers what the digital revolution is to consumers (2020: 30–31). So let us summarize the main phases of his analysis of the consumer's voice, because through this evolution we can better understand what is going on in wine and alcohol e-marketing today.

The voice of the consumer is at the heart of the market relationship between consumers and companies. Any discussion of marketing without the voice of the consumer would be lacking in theoretical value, especially given the changes brought about by the Internet revolution (Kucuk, 2020: 23). From a traditional marketing perspective, a person without purchasing power and willingness can be defined as a silent consumer and a silent market actor (Kucuk, 2020: 22). On the

M. Ramšak, *Social Impact of Wine Marketing*, Contributions to Management Science, https://doi.org/10.1007/978-3-030-89224-1_2

other hand, a consumer who has no idea what to buy or who has an uninformed and uncompromised demand can be defined as a consumer who lives in the void as he has no idea about market dynamics and value systems. In this context, a consumer who has knowledge, experience, and purchasing power but does not want to share his/her positive or negative views can be defined as a silent consumer. Such consumers may see no need or opportunity to express their views to other like-minded consumers, businesses, and even legal entities. Such silence is not good news for markets, as potential buyers can easily become victims of unethical business practices. Another dimension in the definition of the traditional consumer is the consumer's willingness to voice their experiences, products, services, and ideas. The absence of this dimension can bring markets to their knees. Therefore, today's consumers should be defined not only by their purchasing power and willingness to buy, but also by their willingness to inform markets by voicing their experiences and stories in markets, as these consumers do not actively influence many purchasing decisions and act as alternative market information agents in today's dynamically changing digital markets. This benefits not only consumers, but also businesses and markets. Any type of consumer expressions and communication (verbal or non-verbal, soft or loud, bitter or sweet) that supports and advocates the well-being of individuals or a group of consumers by providing reliable information about products and services should be considered as consumer's voice. Such voices generally aim to support consumer well-being and dignity, as well as corporate socially responsible business practices. Therefore, companies are expected to listen to the consumer's voice and understand consumer expectations and/or integrate this consumer voice into their business philosophy. This, in turn, provides companies with healthy market growth and a long-lasting positive consumer-firm relationship, and thus the company's presence in the markets (Kucuk, 2020: 22–23).

In the age of production, the silence of the consumer implies the nonexistence of the consumer in the markets, or at least the assumption that the consumer is not part of the value creation system in the market and thus passively accepts whatever is put before him by the company. This suggests a very autocratic relationship between company and consumers in markets where consumers have no power or voice to reflect their views. In the early 1900s, consumers were in the dark most of the time because there were few purchasing options and there was no sound and truthful market information mechanism from which consumers could obtain reliable information about the products and services produced in the markets. Consumers made their decisions based on very limited or almost no information about the production of the products/services. There was almost no legal regulation to protect consumer voice and complaint behaviors. Thus, the production era can also be defined as "consumer silence" as there was no consumer voice or at least no actively functioning consumer voice in the markets and everything was controlled by the company and only for the benefit of the company (Kucuk, 2020: 24). To keep production levels stable during the slowly cooling economy after the war, producers had to find new buyers and markets. During this time, consumers had more options and a better chance to access better products in the markets. In this era, consumers were able to choose products for themselves, but mostly based on the information that was selectively provided by sellers. The product information introduced with various sales tactics were sometimes misleading and unreliable as selling products was the ultimate goal of marketing efforts rather than producing better-functioning products and services for consumers to satisfy their needs. Therefore, this period in marketing history is commonly referred to as the "sales era." In this era, the goal of marketing shifted from stimulating consumer needs to manipulating consumer needs for the sake of sales and profits. Marketing got its bad reputation from the sales techniques developed in this era. The voice of consumers naturally focuses on the manipulations and unethical sales techniques of the companies of that era. However, there was no mechanism for voting in the markets unless you heard feedback about the products and sellers from people in your own circles. In other words, the consumer voice was not yet active and had no place in the design and production philosophy of companies. The consumer's voice is degraded and consumer complaints had minimal impact on overall market relations because consumers had no place to go to discuss and disseminate such unethical sales practices the way marketers advertise their products. During this time, many consumers realized that there needed to be a strong voice of marketing in the markets to balance the potential power imbalance between consumers and companies. Consumers struggled to find their voice as they were confronted for the first time with widespread unethical marketing practices on this scale. It was during this time that the government had to step in to regulate unethical and harmful business practices that harmed consumers. Ultimately, this was the first step in democratizing the relationship between consumers and businesses for the benefit of consumers and better functioning markets. This is the era when consumer's voice was first placed under the protection of government, and thus this era is called "legalized" or "legitimized voice" (Kucuk, 2020: 25–26).

In the 1970s, product catalogs and face-to-face sales tactics began to be replaced by TV advertisements. As the range of products and services in the markets grew in the 1970s, TV reached the masses of consumers as a new sales tool. Consumers were exposed to more products and services, but communication on TV is a one-way street, and consumer feedback never returned because TV was also heavily controlled by corporations. During this time, the positive voices of consumers were the most desired, as the negative voices were stuck in personal conversations. Although consumers exercised their "right to be heard" and complained to federal agencies about deceptive business practices and perhaps organized protests, the consumer's voice was never able to bypass the powerful broadcast filters of corporations to influence larger crowds. Thus, the only way to raise the voice of consumers was to organize protests and boycotts, thus developing a "collective voice" to oppose corporations engaging in deceptive and unethical marketing practices. Consumers were able to unite and protest against some unethical business practices and bad products by using their social power revealed as collective movements, but consumers were still powerless against corporate media power to reach the masses and change their consumer behavior in their favor. It is clear that consumer voice and consumption are not separate, and therefore consumer voice can only be heard to the extent that they influence consumption (Kucuk, 2020: 26). As a result, in the 1970s, marketers realized for the first time that consumers could also have a collective power to change the consumption direction and market relationship by leaving the markets and raising their voices. However, consumers were not yet equipped with effective communication and transmission tools to convey their message and voice their concerns as independent and individual market actors. It was also very difficult at that time to reach out to the masses and organize them with one voice for a common cause. Although companies increased their efforts to listen to and understand consumers by developing various marketing research tools, the consumer voice again remained stuck in the footnotes of marketing research reports and is not valued by marketers in practice. Although consumer's voice gained prominence in business philosophy from the 1970s to the 1990s, the translation of consumer's voice into business implications was not done sufficiently to tap into consumer voice insights. This era is commonly referred to as the "market era." Companies began listening to their consumers to better understand market demand. In other words, companies used consumer voice mostly for their own benefit and not always for the benefit of consumers. At that time, the majority of marketing scholars defined consumers as the most important market players and actually referred to them as "King" for the benefit of the company. With the shift from slave status in the production era to king status in the market era, consumers had very limited power to control the voice of the market. Although consumers were referred to as king in marketing discussions, in reality, they were almost powerless against corporate marketing machines. This was the irony of the market era, the insincerity of corporations for the purpose of benefit, not the good of the market (Kucuk, 2020: 27–28).

With the Internet revolution in the late 1990s, the trend finally changed in favor of consumers. In the beginning, the Internet is used as an effective shopping tool, but later consumers realize that they can also use the Internet to access social networks, groups, and society to communicate with each other and convey their message. Thus, the Internet created a new forum for public expression and helped consumers rally around important market issues and voice their opinions. With social networking sites on the Internet, consumers finally achieved a very active and exercisable voice. In this era, voice is seen as one of the most important sources of consumer power resulting from changes in technological, social, and legal systems in this new digital world. Internet technology provides price transparency, it is easy for individual consumers to maximize their outcomes by switching to cheaper deals, therefore they are economically empowered in the digital world. These technological advances also made it easier to organize collective anti-consumer movements, which can be seen as social consumer power. With improved language, equality as a result of advances in Internet technology, and the creation of consumer-created online community identities, consumers are empowered to develop their own alternatives to marketer-generated brand identities and values. In this way, consumer voice is not only a mechanism for expressing preferences online, but also a way for responsible and ethical individuals committed to society's collective value system to express themselves. In the 2000s, many consumers began using user-generated media tools to protest corporate misconduct through their own blogs, social networks, and videos. Technologically, the Internet introduced a nonhierarchical distributed network system that allows all parties to have equal status in the networked structure. Strictly technologically, the individual is now on equal footing with the corporation—the corporation has a website and so does the consumer. In other words, the Internet is a technologically transforming platform where free speech, or voice, can be easily exercised (Kucuk, 2020: 28–30). This was truly the new era where consumers began to take control of the voice of the marketplace. Companies that recognized this shift early on sought to integrate the consumer voice on their corporate websites and on social media platforms with online discussion pages to gain the consumer's voice and influence the direction of market conversations. Basically, companies opened up their operations to consumers and sought to bring the company's views into the market conversation. It was in this era that consumer voice first gained importance in business systems, as consumers could raise their voices and influence other like-minded consumers, third parties, the government, and thus the market conversation as a whole. However, such equality of voice was limited only to those with computers and access to the Internet, as well as the knowledge of how to use this new technology. Without consumer access to market information and the ability to raise their voice, consumers who were outside the digital world were at serious risk. The companies, for the first time realized the power of electronic word-of-mouth (e-WOM), which can reach an unlimited number of people in a short period of time and can devastate a company's image and brand equity compared to traditional word-of-mouth in this era. The birth of voice-based consumer power forced businesses to listen more to their consumers, drastically changing their traditional business mentality. Some tried to contend with this emerging consumer power to protect their consumer value systems, while others wisely focused on finding a way to integrate consumer voice into their own systems to capitalize on raw and true consumer culture. Thus, one of the most important lessons learned from the Internet era is the convergence between consumers and businesses and the reintegration of consumers into business systems. Some companies have rediscovered their loyal consumers in a variety of ways. In some cases, the company's loyal consumers began to work for the company as their own employees. Many companies are trying to capitalize on consumer creativity and innovation. Some companies began to use online consumer communities that they developed under their domain and use such online communities to recruit, educate, and assist new consumers with product and service issues. This ultimately reduces consumer support expenses and increases consumer satisfaction to the benefit of the company. The more corporate voice lost its market power to consumer's voice, the more desperate some companies became and started hiring ordinary consumers to deliver their own version of market messages through them. This was the birth of a new kind of consumer's voice: paid consumer voice (or "paid bloggers"). Since such consumers are paid to review products/services for others, this cannot be defined as a true representation of consumer's voice, as some others referred to this practice as bribing consumers for the benefit of the company. In addition, some companies also used automated voices to imitate consumer voices to introduce their secret agenda in the markets (Kucuk, 2020: 31–33).

With the advent of smartphones in the 2010s, consumer's voice entered a new phase. In this era, consumers can easily access the digital world with smartphones as majority of consumers can use various smartphone options that have broadband features to access the digital world 24/7. Smartphones are easier to carry than computers, but offer almost the functionality of a computer with their computer-like high storage capacities. Thus, most of the digital divide problems caused by lack of access to technology, especially computers, were solved in this singularity era. Moreover, smartphones offered consumers easy-to-use features and conveniences. The technological knowledge required to use smartphones is very low for anyone (regardless of age). This was not the case during the Internet era as it was difficult to access the digital world without prior experience and computer skills. The digitalization of markets has reached a high level with smartphone technology. Consumers can be anywhere, anytime to share their stories and influence other like-minded consumers in real time. Consumers can now access their social networks, like-minded fellow consumers and millions of others without effort as automated systems inform them simultaneously. Consumers can literally feel their power at their fingertips. The speed of information sharing and the proliferation of consumer voices in markets is such that companies are now falling behind when it comes to listening and understanding what consumers are saying and how to counter such consumer voices. Today's consumers are behaving like individual media broadcasters, walking around with their smartphone camera in hand, recording everything, reporting, and informing a huge crowd of viewers at all times. Videos, stories, and images flood the digital public space for consumption by other like-minded consumers. Every product and service is instantly reviewed and tagged by consumer review and complaint sites using rich media tools. The entire digital market have now become giant consumer voice rating systems. So with the increasing inclusion of real-time consumer voices in today's markets, consumers are dominantly shaping market opinion while marketers are running out of steam. In this environment, companies are no longer scandal-proof and when something goes wrong for a company, it is heard immediately in consumer markets. Companies are now constantly being watched by consumers 24 hours a day. In some cases, these consumers are reaching and influencing society faster than professional media outlets. Consumers are no longer passive recipients or even ordinary voicers of their complaints, rather they are active broadcasters, newsmakers, storytellers, and as such, they control the markets with their voices, keeping the pulse of the public and threatening the economic livelihood of businesses. Now companies need consumers not only to consume their products and services, but also for their propaganda and voice power to survive in today's challenging markets. In this singularity era, consumers can dominate market communications with their version of stories. This in turn has led to a very noisy market as it has become very difficult to distinguish what is right, wrong, true, or fake. Hence, this era can also be termed as the "noisy era" as there are no tools and regulations to pass through such noise bubbles created by various third parties. The word that best describes this new type of consumers would be "voicing consumers" or hence the combination of these two words

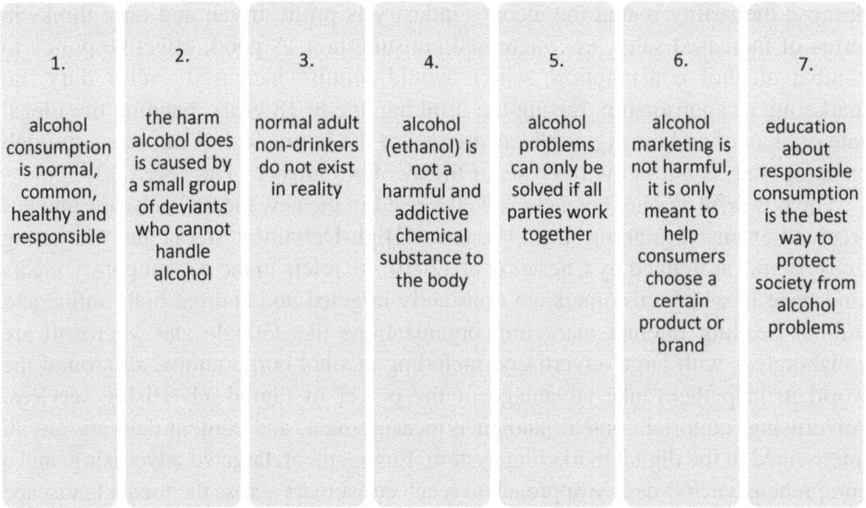

Fig. 2.1 The seven pillars of half-truths and lies of the alcohol industry about the harmful effects of drinking. Source: Designed by Mojca Ramšak 2021 (for the text see: The seven 2011)

"voicesumers." Voicesumers are the loudest consumers we have ever seen in the history of marketing (Kucuk, 2020: 35–36, 38, 39–40).

The voice of the consumer is parallel by a voice, or rather many voices, of the alcohol industry. As the European Centre for Monitoring Alcohol Marketing warns, it is important to note that the alcohol industry, as well as the advertising and retail industries, continually seek to prevent disclosure of information about the harmful effects of consumption of alcohol by deliberately ignoring or denying the important and harmful effects of drinking (The seven 2011). The alcohol industry sends subversive messages that are, at their core, half-truths or outright lies about the harmful effects of drinking. Such messages are: alcohol consumption is normal, common, healthy, and very responsible; the harm alcohol does is caused by a small group of deviants who cannot handle alcohol; normal adult non-drinkers do not exist in reality; alcohol (ethanol) is not a harmful and addictive chemical substance to the body; alcohol problems can only be solved if all parties work together; alcohol marketing is not harmful, it is only meant to help consumers choose a certain product or brand; education about responsible consumption is the best way to protect society from alcohol problems. These "arguments" and biased representations are communication tools to defend alcohol products and prevent or delay legal restrictions (The seven 2011). The reader can also see a visual representation of these pillars in Fig. 2.1.

Therefore, in traditional marketing and on the Internet through alcohol advertising, alcohol consumption is almost always portrayed and associated with health, sportsmanship, physical beauty, romance, having friends, and leisure activities. The fact that alcohol is also associated with serious health problems, road accidents, unemployment, violence, child abuse, and suicide is never seen in advertising because the reality is that the alcohol industry is profit driven and only thinks in terms of increased sales, i.e., increased consumption. A good, effective policy to combat alcohol consumption, which would require increased excise duty, no marketing or sponsorship, raising the drinking age to 18 years, banning the illegal sale of alcohol and raising public awareness of the harm alcohol can cause through campaigning, is not in the interests of the alcohol industry (The seven 2011).

The powerful alcohol business is well-versed in the new media landscape and has received extensive training in it. The term "High-Definition Media and Marketing Ecosystem," as defined by Chester et al. (2010: 4), refers to the contemporary media landscape in which customers are constantly targeted and courted both online and offline. Leading Internet marketing organizations like Google and Microsoft are collaborating with large advertisers, including alcohol corporations, all around the world to help them take advantage of the power of digital advertising services. Advertising, editorial content, audience measurement, and content delivery are all intertwined in the digital marketing system. Engagement, targeted advertising, and a comprehensive 360-degree approach to reach consumers across the media landscape are three features that define this new paradigm (Chester et al., 2010: 4).

Engagement, which is defined as a subtle, subconscious process in which consumers begin to integrate the ad's ideas with their own connections, symbols, and metaphors to make the brand more personally relevant, is one of the core concepts propelling the evolution of interactive marketing. The idea is to create an environment in which consumers are genuinely interacting with the brand, befriending the product, and integrating it into their personal and social interactions, rather than simply exposing them to a product or service. Creating subconscious associations with brands is also a part of engagement. In order to gain a better understanding of the level of involvement, interaction, intimacy, and influence a customer has for or with a brand over time, alcoholic beverage companies, ad agencies, and private research firms that work with alcoholic beverage companies are developing methods for fostering and measuring such engagement. Alcohol marketers may increase online engagement by including material that their target audience will want to spend time with. Alcohol companies collaborate with digital marketing branded page development and management experts to create marketing connected environments that promote products in a variety of ways, including discussion boards, polls and quizzes, videos, photos, links to offsite promotions, and custom-developed applications. Marketers are increasingly turning to tactics from the burgeoning discipline of neuromarketing, which aims to figure out how precise patterns of brain activation predict purchasing, as well as the brain's potential shopping centers and the neurological foundation of purchasing. Advertisement campaigns are judged not only on their visibility but also on their engagement. Furthermore, many digital ad agencies are paid only if they deliver relevant, meaningful connections between customers and brands, as evidenced by measurable online behaviors like entering information, writing reviews, voting, sharing, or interacting with brand-focused content (Chester et al., 2010: 4–5).

Companies can use *behavioral targeting* to build one-of-a-kind, long-term relationships with their clients. Marketers can build individualized marketing and sales appeals based on a customer's unique tastes, actions, and psychological profile through continual data collecting and tracking. They are looking at how frequently and for how long users buy the product. The most crucial aspect of digital strategy is attracting new clients to loyalty programs. A loyalty program will assist you in identifying and retaining your most devoted clients. Many initiatives try to encourage consumers to disclose personal information including phone numbers, email addresses, and preferences (Chester et al., 2010: 5).

The *360-degree approach*, one of the most important aspects of modern marketing, strives to reach viewers and users frequently, wherever they are in the media landscape, both online and offline. Marketers create campaigns to capitalize on people's constant access to technology, multitasking habits, and the fluidity of their media experiences. Residential broadband adoption, the rise of the mobile Web and wireless networks, and services like instant messaging and texting have all contributed to the creation of an always-on media experience. Major media businesses are now offering cross-platform marketing opportunities, in which marketers can target people across all of the company's media holdings, both online and offline, with a single purchase. The rapid rise of new services, such as mobile video and mobile social networks, is being fueled by Internet-enabled cell phones, many of which are ad-supported (Chester et al., 2010: 5).

The numerous advertising strategies and technology are not independent of one another. Advertisers use a variety of strategies. Many strategies (engagement, targeted advertising, and the 360-degree approach) and platforms (social media, online video, mobile, networks, and immersive media/virtual reality) come into play concurrently, especially in new media, where contextual and commercial boundaries are very porous. Because it is a channel via which information about businesses, products, and services travels, social media has had a huge impact on marketing.

Marketing messages are quickly disseminated to networks of friends and acquaintances via social media, and through them to their acquaintances, enhancing persuasiveness. The alcohol business is keeping a close eye on consumer perceptions of alcohol products and the impact of social media on sales. Alcohol marketers profile social media users because they provide so much information about themselves, allowing them to be addressed with great precision based on their requirements. Surveys, virtual awards, free samples, quizzes, Internet board games, various alcohol-related trivia, blogs, and other market tactics spreading on social media are just a few examples (Chester et al., 2010: 6–9, 13). The new wine industry makes use of new media that is easy to create (YouTube, Twitter, Facebook, podcasts), and where speed and mobility are important. With the use of digital resources to supplement analogue history, new or beginning wineries can compete with established ones. Much of this creative industries expansion is concentrated in cities, with the goal of attracting a 'creative class' and bohemians who will fuel branding, skill development, and design (Brabazon et al., 2014: 87).

Technological advances through digital media provide new opportunities and new ways for actors to reach, influence, and interact with consumers, especially young people. This is achieved through a combination of paid media (such as pop-up ads or commercials), owned media (branded websites and social media pages), and co-created content with users. Marketing through these new media channels can be targeted to specific audiences, spread virally among users, and accessed in almost any context via smartphones, and can actively recruit users into the marketing process. Digital marketing is more powerful and less controllable than traditional alcohol marketing (Brummer et al., 2019: 32). Alcohol is marketed on Facebook with many photos, videos, longer recordings, and blogs, shorter notices and individual photos on Twitter. YouTube and Instagram are important media especially because of their visual impact. Instagram is used by winemakers to show photos of their wine cellars, photos of unloading a stock of bottles of wine in front of a warehouse, or other everyday chores. One or two photos a day at different times and a short one- or two-minute video are enough to keep the attention of followers. In the last decade, e-sales of wine have expanded in social media, which are already used by more than 90% of winegrowers and winemakers.

Clearly, online advertising differs significantly from traditional advertising. The Internet has created a unique mode of communication that falls between mass and individual communication. The Internet is also a very appealing advertising medium because it offers unique marketing characteristics that are not available in other forms of media such as newspapers, radio, television, and so on. Many advertising prohibitions on certain products or services may be found in EU law. However, no extensive laws would apply to online advertising. Product limits are intended to prevent the promotion of items or services that are damaging to people's health or that breach universally accepted ethical norms.

Alcohol, tobacco, and prescription pharmaceuticals are generally excluded from advertising, whereas the advertising of paramedications necessitates the display of specific, clear information to the user in order for them to be used properly. These rules apply to all forms of online advertising (Nowak-Gruca, 2018: 42).

The issue of Internet advertising is complicated because the recipient has virtually no way of avoiding the advertised content, which distinguishes the recipient of e-advertising from the recipient of an advertisement via other electronic media, who can choose whether or not to "receive" the advertisement on his or her own. The recipient of online advertising is frequently unaware of the legal standards that govern the industry. Online advertising aims to hold the recipient's attention for as long as possible, and it has far more capabilities in this regard than traditional types of advertising. The most intrusive forms of advertising should be seen as breaking the standards of fair competition in this situation (Nowak-Gruca, 2018: 42).

References

Brabazon, T., Winter, M., & Gandy, B. (2014). *Digital wine. How QR codes facilitate new Markets for Small Wine Industries*. Springer Briefs in Business.

Brummer, J., Schölin, L., Neufeld, M., Ferreira-Borges, C. (2019). Alcohol control policy in the EU+. Status report on alcohol consumption, harm and policy responses in 30 European countries 2019. *Status report on alcohol consumption, harm and policy responses in 30 European countries 2019*. Copenhagen: World Health Organization, pp. 25–37. Retrieved

August 24, 2021 from https://www.euro.who.int/__data/assets/pdf_file/0019/411418/Alcohol-consumption-harm-policy-responses-30-European-countries-2019.pdf

Chester, J., Montgomery, K., & Dorfman, L. (2010). Alcohol marketing in the digital age. In *Berkeley media studies group*. Retrieved August 24, 2021 from http://www.digitalads.org/documents/BMSG-CDD-Digital-Alcohol-Marketing.pdf

Kucuk, S. U. (2020). *Consumer voice: The democratization of consumption Markets in the Digital age*. Palgrave Macmillan.

Nowak-Gruca, A. (2018). Selected legal problems of online advertising. *Lexonomica, 10*(1), 33–44. Retrieved August 24, 2021 from https://journals.um.si/index.php/lexonomica/article/view/114/79

The Seven Key Messages of the Alcohol Industry: Information for Everyone Who Wants to be Aware of the Real Intentions of the Alcohol Industry. (2011). Addiction Info Switzerland (Switzerland), AV-OG-TIL (Norway), Boozerebellion; Friends of Temperance (Finland), Deutsche Hauptstelle für Suchtfragen (Germany), Dutch Institute for Alcohol Policy (STAP, The Netherlands), Eurocare Italia (Italy), IOGT-NTO (Sweden), Landsraadet (Denmark), Marin Institute – San Rafael (USA), State Agency for Prevention of Alcohol-Related Problems (PARPA; Poland), Vereniging voor Alcohol en andere Drugproblemen (VAD; België). Retrieved August 24, 2021, from https://eucam.info/wp-content/uploads/2014/04/seven_key_messages_of_the_alcohol_industry.pdf

Chapter 3
Wine Storytelling

It is the wine that leads me on, the wild wine that sets the wisest man to sing at the top of his lungs, laugh like a fool – it drives the man to dancing. . .it even tempts him to blurt out stories better never told.

Homer, The Odyssey

Abstract This chapter introduces us to the concept and practice of e-storytelling in the wine industry as one of the most powerful marketing tools that can be both brand and customer driven; the relationship between wine storytelling and wine tourism destination storytelling; the people who make the wine and their family stories; and the most common technical options in wine storytelling. Digital storytelling is more than just using technology; it is a way of communicating, integrating, and imagining. Wine is a product unlike any other in wine tourism, inextricably linked to the region, its soil, climate, and geomorphology, as well as the local people, their history, traditional cultivation methods, taste, and culture. As a result, sharing the story of a winery is inextricably linked to sharing the story of a wine tourism destination.

Successful forms of e-marketing like to include elements of experience economy with active participatory, collaborative, and sensory experience (Pine & Gilmore, 1998). In addition to social media, thoughtfully advertised viticulture and winemaking family stories are also important for distinguishing wine brands. Nostalgia and reliving feelings from the past and exploiting elements of the wine-growing heritage are powerful marketing tools.

The impact of e-storytelling on various aspects of communication, particularly content marketing strategy, is widely recognized in the digital era. Digital storytelling is more than just using technology; it is "a medium of expression, communication, integration, and imagination" (Malita & Martin, 2010: 3061 in: Bonarou et al., 2019: 81–82). In the marketing literature, researchers emphasize the storytelling approach as a technique for framing information in an understandable, meaningful, and memorable way, as well as an effective and influential technique for shaping

M. Ramšak, *Social Impact of Wine Marketing*, Contributions to Management Science, https://doi.org/10.1007/978-3-030-89224-1_3

brands and creating emotional investment on both a corporate and a product level (Bonarou et al., 2019: 82). Storytelling, as a business concept, has a significant impact on how companies can build strong corporate cultures and credible brands (Fog et al., 2010 in: Bonarou et al., 2019: 82). According to Jiwa (2016), "people don't buy what you do; they buy how you make them feel and the story you give them to tell. If you don't have a story you are just another commodity." A brand story, on the other hand, is more than just content and a narrative on a website or text in a brochure: "Your story isn't just what you tell people; it's also what they believe about you based on the signals your brand sends. The story is a complete picture made up of facts, feelings, and interpretations, which means that a part of your story isn't even told by you" (Jiwa, 2016 in Bonarou et al., 2019: 82–83).

There are two types of stories: those told by the enterprise (brand-centric) and those told by its customers (customer-centric). Brand-centric stories emphasize visual branding by presenting the enterprise or product at its best moments and in real-world situations, whereas key product messages emphasize what the audience can expect (e.g., events, packages, and offers). Customer-centric stories, on the other hand, are related to the in-the-moment experiences that customers evaluate and share about the product, services, or destination. Two preconditions are proposed for the consumer to be immersed in the story and have an extraordinary experience: "one is the need for the experience to take place in a hedonic service consumption setting, and the other is a servicescape that allows the consumer to step away from everyday reality" (Mossberg, 2008 in: Bonarou et al., 2019: 83).

Wine, in the case of wine tourism, is a product unlike any other, inextricably linked to the region, its terroir/soil, climate, and geomorphology, while also inextricably linked to the local people, their history, traditional cultivation methods, taste, and culture. As a result, telling the story of a winery cannot be separated from telling the story of a wine tourism destination. Wineries are components of a wine region, and a wine region cannot be successful unless its wineries are well-known and successful. Each sip of wine not only fills the mouth with flavor, but also the mind and soul with images and sentiments. Furthermore, wine storytelling is difficult to separate from the people who make the wine. According to Herskovitz and Crystal (2010), every story requires a clearly defined central character with whom people can identify and form a long-lasting emotional bond. In the wine industry, this "strong brand persona" is the winemaker; and a winemaker battling the elements of nature, for example, can be considered a strong motif that leads to high emotional engagement with the audience. Wine (-tourism) stories imply a link between the winery and its products and specific mythological, historical, folkloric, geographical, and cultural heritage narratives. Stories that are linked to other success stories are undeniably an important key factor in enticing tourism storytelling (Bonarou et al., 2019: 83–84).

Part of the family stories also includes a common form of marketing, a virtual vineyard, with interesting videos and photos of landscapes, vineyards, and vines in all their varietal diversity, tasks in the vineyard, harvesting, wine pressing, pouring wine, storage, visual comparisons between the same tasks over time, etc. Besides, Internet videos distributed by crowds of social media users reach a larger audience and are always accessible and much cheaper on YouTube than ads on television. They are easy to record with mobile phones and later edited into visually and audibly shorter films of various lengths.

Wine websites also allow consumers to engage in sharing their experiences and impressions of the wine they have bought. Their ratings and critiques allow winemakers to find out firsthand what customers want about their wine.

There are also free mobile wine apps with maps of regions, winemakers, locations of wine shops and restaurants, digital wine routes or real wine events such as wine tastings and wine fairs, apps for recognizing QR Codes (Quick Response Codes) on labels, animation apps wine labels, applications with wine ratings and personalized recommendations for purchase according to the user's taste, applications for purchasing wine with door-to-door delivery, applications for organizing and pricing one's wine archive collection and those recommending the best wine and food combinations or otherwise advising about the culture of drinking wine.[1] Marketing alcohol through smartphones is an extremely powerful tool as it involves both behavioral and location targeting of consumers. Some of the phone apps are also adapted for visually impaired people, with links to Facebook, Twitter, Instagram, and other social networks used by winegrowers and sellers, they show the growth of their capital and links to other related apps.

References

Bonarou, C., Tsartas, P., & Sarantakou, E. (2019). E-storytelling and wine tourism branding: Insights from the "wine roads of northern Greece". In M. Sigala, N. Richard, & S. Robinson (Eds.), *Wine tourism destination management and marketing: Theory and cases* (pp. 77–98). Palgrave Macmillan.

Fog, K., Budtz, C., Munch, P., & Blanchette, S. (2010). *Storytelling: Branding in practice*. Springer.

Herskovitz, S. E., & Crystal, M. (2010). The essential brand persona: Storytelling and branding. *Journal of Business Strategy, 31*(3), 21–28. Retrieved August 24, 2021 from https://www.emerald.com/insight/content/doi/10.1108/02756661011036673/full/html

Jiwa, B. (2016). Brand story strategy. *The story of telling*. Retrieved August 24, 2021 from http://thestoryoftelling.com/brand-story-strategy

Malita, L., & Martin, C. (2010). Digital storytelling as web passport to success in the 21st century. *Social and Behavioral Sciences, 2*, 3060–3064.

Mossberg, L. (2008). Extraordinary experiences through storytelling. *Scandinavian Journal of Hospitality and Tourism, 8*(3), 195–210. Retrieved August 24, 2021 from https://www.tandfonline.com/doi/abs/10.1080/15022250802532443

Pine, J. B. II, & Gilmore, J. H. (1998, July, August). Welcome to the experience economy. *Harvard Business Review*. Retrieved August 24, 2021 from https://hbr.org/1998/07/welcome-to-the-experience-economy

[1] For example: Delectable, Banquet, Vivino, Hello Vino, Drizly, Wine-Searcher, Wine Ring, Wine Picker, Winc Wines, WineRatings+, Wine Enthusiast Tasting Guide, Cellar Tracker, CorkageFee, Wine Events, Winery Passport.

Chapter 4
Wearable Technology and Wine

It doesn't stop being magic just because you know how it works.

Terry Pratchett, The Wee Free Men

Abstract Wearable technology, which can act as a link between the customer and digital alcohol marketing, is the topic of this chapter. By improving reality with Artificial Intelligence, e-commerce, mobile apps, and artificial intelligence have the ability to radically revolutionize the business model. From a wine storytelling standpoint, wearable technology examples are utilized to demonstrate the distinction between Augmented Reality and Virtual Reality.

Wearable technology in the alcohol industry refers to two different things. First, it can be a device or devices that serve as a link between the consumer—buyer or drinker—and digital marketing for alcohol that augments reality and provides a new experience in buying and drinking alcohol. Second, it is a device for preventive and curative purposes with transdermal alcohol sensors or mobile-connected breathalyzers that measure how much alcohol someone has drunk and are used in healthcare and criminal justice to detect alcohol use.

The importance of wearable technology in terms of a reality-enhancing device aimed at increasing sales could be explained by factors influencing alcohol marketing.

Namely, when the right product is offered in the right place, at the right price, and at the right time, the messages to the consumer are crystal clear (Gibson, 2021). When marketing, advertising and sales campaigns emphasize these four pillars—namely, product (including services), price, place, and promotion—customers have enough information to compare products with those of competitors. With today's digital marketing technologies that include e-commerce, apps, and artificial intelligence, companies can significantly strengthen the four pillars and expand their advertising reach. Popular digital marketing concepts have not influenced the four

M. Ramšak, *Social Impact of Wine Marketing*, Contributions to Management Science, https://doi.org/10.1007/978-3-030-89224-1_4

pillars because they were developed long before the Internet. This does not mean that current popular marketing concepts such as search engine optimization, social media marketing, and algorithmic targeted advertising should replace the four pillars, but they can be integrated into campaign strategies, especially if those campaigns use Artificial Intelligence tools available in the market. In a sense, digital marketing can be considered an extension of the last pillar, advertising. Nevertheless, e-commerce and Artificial Intelligence have the ability to redefine the entire business model and reshape the organizational processes of companies from top to bottom. Artificial Intelligence also makes it easy to add an additional "P" to the original four pillars. In addition to product, price, place, and promotion, we now have "people" as a fifth pillar. By empowering Artificial Intelligence-driven digital marketing software to handle the modern 5-pillar system that puts the customer at the center of the marketing strategy, alcohol companies can take advantage of Artificial Intelligence (Gibson, 2021).

Focusing on the customer has never been more possible—thanks to Artificial Intelligence, collected customer data, and customer-centric, targeted advertising campaigns. By putting customers and their specific needs at the center of marketing efforts, the business model naturally redefines itself. The use of technology solutions such as customer data collection, list segmentation, and outreach automation with emails, text messages, and app push notifications adds a highly personalized touch to marketing efforts. Because these technologies use built-in Artificial Intelligence that collects customer data relevant to their browsing and purchase history, the automated product suggestions that go out to customers speak directly to their interests, making promotional offers all the more likely to be noticed. This technology can significantly accelerate sales and help liquor retailers, bar owners, and alcohol distribution center sales staff better target customer groups and successfully increase sales (Gibson, 2021).

Augmented Reality that brought the digital into the store is a special kind of wine storytelling. The difference between Augmented Reality and Virtual Reality lies in the experience of the real world and the imagined world, which are not the same. In Virtual Reality, the software builds an entirely new virtual world; in Augmented Reality the real world is seen with additional information projected virtually onto the display of a wearable device. Reality is enriched, enhanced, or extended with virtual information. Augmented Reality Wine storytelling, for example, animates and makes the alcoholic beverage a rich experience while engaging the mind and taste buds.

Wearable technologies in the alcohol industry became popular in 2014 when Google launched Google Glass, part of a new wave of wearable technologies in the United Kingdom. Google Glasses could be used in a variety of ways in the drinks world (Ross, 2014). For example, it could be used to scan barcodes and reveal data. All you needed to do is take a bottle off the shelf and use Glass' built-in camera to scan the barcode on the bottle without using your hands. Then you could compare prices and see all sorts of information about the brand without dropping your purchase. Google Glass could also overlay images and information on top of the customer's view of the real world in front of them: that's Augmented Reality.

Wineries and distilleries could allow their customers to launch videos about their brands right in the store—sweeping views of their vineyards, whisky coming out of the distillery, or a virtual winemaker standing in front of the customer describing their wine. Alternatively, stores could have their customers look along the wine shelves and messages would pop up in front of the best deals and most appropriate selections based on the customer's purchase history. Busy bartenders could receive cocktail orders directly to their Glass, without having to put a bottle down. Wearing Google Glass, and with the World Lens app, the customer could simply look at the back label of a bottle or a bar menu and get it translated instantly—it appears in real time overlaid with what users are looking at. The built-in camera in Glass could take social sharing to a new level—users do not just take photos of the food; they record an entire video while enjoying the cocktail. One of Google's original videos promoting the Glass shows a trip to Napa Valley as an example. On the Glass, the traveler gets directions, can access information about individual wineries, pop in augmented reality videos of what the vineyards look like at different times of the year, and see the winery itself in the midst of a busy harvest. Consultants and winemakers could see what's happening from a colleague's point of view in real time, and offer real-time advice. A worker in the winery or vineyard wearing Glass could share what they are doing and get instant advice on what to do next. The user could "meet the winemaker" in an interview and watch the winemaker talk and have a live view of what he or she is doing—that is, watch the winemaking, blending, and grape selection process from the winemaker's perspective, with additional live commentary from the winemaker. Since sound and color in certain combinations help to enhance the taste of the wine glass, projecting a certain color of light through the lens and matching music through the earpiece could help to create that mood. Finally, retail could change when staff wears Glass. Although facial recognition technology is explicitly banned, retailers could recognize customers as they enter a store and project their favorite purchase onto the employee's Glass screen to offer timely recommendations (Ross, 2014).

References

Gibson, M. (2021). How technology is reshaping the liquor industry. *FasTrax*. Retrieved August 24, 2021 from https://www.goftx.com/blogs/posts/how-technology-is-reshaping-the-liquor-industry

Ross, R. (2014, 25 June). 10 uses for google glass and drinks. *The Drinks Business*. Retrieved August 24, 2021 from https://www.thedrinksbusiness.com/2014/06/10-uses-for-google-glass-and-drinks/

Chapter 5
Smart Packaging: The Labels Come to Life

There is truth in wine, but you never see it listed in the ingredients on the label.

Josh Stern

Abstract Smart packaging, particularly smart bottle labels, is one sort of wearable technology. Because alcohol labeling requirements differ widely around the world, the chapter begins by describing the various regulations that have been implemented in the wine, spirits, and aromatized wine industries, as well as noting that Interactive Technologies, particularly Virtual and Augmented Reality, are not adequately regulated in the alcohol industry. The notion and purpose of luxury products are used to further explain the personalizing of alcohol sales. The chapter also looks at QR codes on labels as a way for a vineyard to send information to a customer, as well as other appealing multisensory wine experiences.

New means of labeling bottles or other packaging contributed to the expansion of wearable technology. The experience of buying and drinking alcoholic beverages was given a new dimension by smart packaging.

Labelling requirements for alcoholic beverages are currently quite variable around the world and rather limited compared to the labelling of food and tobacco products. Alcohol labelling requirements are implemented nationally and internationally through one or a combination of means, including laws and codes for food standards and voluntary agreements between industry and government. Some countries have introduced mandatory health labels on alcoholic beverages with the aim to reduce the negative consequences of drinking and alcohol intoxication. National food labelling laws exist within a network of international conventions and agreements that impose obligations on countries that are signatories to them (Alcohol labelling, 2017: 2, 3).

The European Commission has adopted several regulations implementing quality schemes for the wine sector, the spirit drinks sector, and the aromatized wine sector.

M. Ramšak, *Social Impact of Wine Marketing*, Contributions to Management Science, https://doi.org/10.1007/978-3-030-89224-1_5

Part of the legislation is intended for the definition, description, labelling, and presentation of certain products in the wine sector and for the protection of geographical indications of spirit drinks and aromatized wine products.

Regulation (EU) No 1151/2012 of European Parliament and of the Council of November 21, 2012, on quality schemes for agricultural products and foodstuffs defines labelling as: "any words, particulars, trademarks, brand name, pictorial matter or symbol relating to a foodstuff and placed on any packaging, document, notice, label, ring or collar accompanying or referring to such foodstuff" (Regulation (EU) No 1151/2012: Article 3, paragraph 4).

The labelling of agricultural products and foodstuffs is subject to the general rules laid down in Directive 2000/13/EC of the European Parliament and of the Council of March 20, 2000, on the approximation of the laws of the Member States relating to the labelling, presentation and advertising of foodstuffs, and in particular the provisions designed to prevent labelling which is likely to confuse or mislead the consumer (Regulation (EU) No 1151/2012: paragraph 8).

The regulation, which came into force in 2019, contains mandatory and optional rules on labelling and presentation, as well as rules on certain bottle shapes and closures. Mandatory rules are established to help consumers better understand the specific character of wine sector products and to guarantee producers recognition of the quality of their products. Labels of wine sector products must include a range of information including: the category of wine product as defined, the term protected designations of origin or protected geographical indications for wines with these designations and their respective names, the actual alcoholic strength by volume, the indication of origin, the indication of the bottler, for sparkling wines the producer or the seller, for imported wines the importer, the sugar content of sparkling wines. Optional information may include the vintage, the grape variety(ies), sugar content (for wines other than sparkling wines), traditional terms for wines with a protected designation of origin or protected geographical indication, EU symbol for a protected designation of origin or protected geographical indication, terms referring to specific production methods, and terms referring to a holding.

In addition, alcoholic beverages have been given special treatment. They are currently exempt from international conventions that regulate all other psychoactive substances, as well as from major food laws that require ingredient labeling and nutritional information. Among the various tools and policy options that could be used to raise awareness of the risks of alcohol abuse, several consumer organizations (such as European Consumer Organization) and public health organizations (such as World Health Organization) have long called for consideration of mandatory ingredient and nutrition labeling and health messages. As a general principle of good governance, citizens should be confident that the food regulatory system designed to protect their health and safety is working effectively. Product labelling regulation is an important tool for promoting healthier habits, and public agencies are ideally positioned to use it (Alcohol labelling, 2017: 10).

Interactive Technologies, especially Virtual and Augmented Reality in the alcohol sector, are not yet regulated by European Union law. From a legal point of view, Interactive Technologies on labels of alcoholic beverages would fall under the optional rules on labelling and presentation. In reality, the development of

Interactive Technologies is many steps ahead of the legal regulations and the following examples prove this statement.

In alcohol industry, labels and packaging enhanced with Augmented Reality transform labels and packaging into a 24/7 interactive customer experience with videos, websites, and mobile app links to engage and educate consumers. Tech Labels is a big investment, especially for family wineries, but Augmented Reality also provides more tools for distribution and is an advantage in the competitive wine industry. Tech labels can be updated seasonally to further tell the stories of wineries and wines. Using "gamification" to engage people in a way that keeps them engaged and inviting customers to find keys and tokens and learn more about the story is not the future, it is a reality (The Wine Industry Advisor, 2019).

The labels contain legally regulated and optional information and thus acts as a medium of communication between the producer and the consumer. Most wines have front labels with basic information (e.g., alcohol content, wine type, and country of origin) and back labels with additional remarks (e.g., serving suggestions) (Behrens et al., 2013: 400).

Only prescribed markings and packaging may be used for the labeling of must, wine and other products (on labels, packaging, documents, and advertising material when offered to the final consumer). These must not mislead the consumer as to the geographical origin, quality, ingredients, vine varieties, possible decorations, producers, specific production methods, and other characteristics of the alcoholic beverage.

Today, luxury wine marketing is fueled by social media and by competition, forcing the wine industry to consider distribution channels that were once considered antithetical to marketing premium brands. In addition to selling quality, one of the most important strategic market trends is personalizing the sale. The goal is to make the consumer feel like the star of the show. Another important aspect is the authenticity of information and stories about the origin of the wine they receive.

If there is one striking aspect of luxury, it is the visible nature of its logos and brands. This is normal. Luxury is the symbolic and hedonistic recompense of success, and therefore of the acquisition of power. Through its logos and brands with their high recognition and visibility, it functions like the medals. This is why luxury must be seen, since one of the sources of recompense is the prestige in the eyes of all, and in particular of peers. By the visibility of the labels—the supports of the brand—is re-updated the function of what was called *étiquette* at the court of French kings Louis XIII and Louis XIV: an obligation to expenditure and show. Luxury is the distinctive sign of their own rarity. As for the logos on the series products, they give additional soul to the products and are an auxiliary means for the consumer to drag themselves above their current condition (Kapferer & Bastien, 2009: 77). In a traditional society, the social order cannot be questioned. In monarchical France, luxury was the obligation of power: *étiquette* was formal rules that regulated consumption and expenditure visible to the court in order to maintain one's position there. It is instructive that we have moved from *étiquette* to the luxury brand, which is written on ostentatious labels (the French word *étiquette* is the exact translation of the English word label). This marker has the function of maintaining rank and visibility of rank. Therefore, it must be highly visible: like a social seal. The French Revolution brought the abolition of privileges, a new ruling class and an egalitarian ideology. More importantly, the British Industrial Revolution brought mass production. Automatically, prices could fall when demand was high. So it was necessary to stimulate demand. The emerging capitalism created new fortunes. Economic power was no longer an inheritance, a right, but something acquired. Through the enrichment associated with labor, one could buy better quality manufactured products. Imitation of power was the lever for more expensive purchases, but also for the appearance on the market of imitations of the objects of power. This imitation of power enabled everyone to rise above their condition, to indulge in pleasures and sensations, to finally become somebody, to stop being just one of "those people" by imitating people who really have power. To exist, one must elevate oneself. This is why the luxury market and its manifestations were born: to provide everyone with the means for a provisional, even fictitious elevation, a fleeting pleasure. We can imitate the signs of wealth without being rich (Kapferer & Bastien, 2009: 78).

Niche strategies that emphasize customization or personalization of products do well in the affluent market. For example, customers are encouraged to design a custom label for their wine bottles. A personalized label applied to a wine bottle can cost several hundred dollars. The task of marketers is to use their creativity to enable customers to personalize the products they want. There can be a pleasant feeling of satisfaction when these personalized products are shown to friends and this also enables inner emotional experiences (Michman & Mazze, 2006: 164).

For the more eccentric adult drinkers (but not necessarily only for them), the wine industry uses Augmented Reality, where the real and virtual worlds are intertwined, which the user observes and listens to via a mobile device or glasses. The technology is mostly used in manufacturing, tourism, and entertainment, but the wine industry also follows this trend. Thus, in Augmented Reality, we can watch and listen to wine labels with the stories of celebrities from the entertainment industry who do not participate in it voluntarily because they are already dead or are fictional. Such branding, introduced in 2017, achieved such recognition in the same year that sales of otherwise average table wines increased by as much as 60%.

A quick scan of QR Code can offer information and features that the producer could not fit on the label. The codes are a way to nurture customer curiosity (Teclemariam, 2019). QR Codes are a good fit for almost any product, but they have a special advantage when it comes to wine (Brabazon et al., 2014: 55). Many people already shop with a phone in hand, whether to look up vintage or text about what's for dinner. QR Codes are useful in grocery stores and places where a wine expert may not be present, and they allow the producer to be part of the conversation (Teclemariam, 2019).

According to Brabazon (Brabazon et al., 2014), when purchasing a bottle of wine, many consumers do not simply purchase the product on the shelf for its intended use; they purchase the product's heritage. Customers who buy wine must be carefully tracked down and analyzed. The customer is frequently interested not only in the wine's future, whether they want to drink it that evening or the following weekend, but also in its past—the grape variety, the vineyard, the winemaker and winery, and the process of the wine went through before it arrived in front of the consumer. Most importantly, they want to know that they are getting good value for their money, that they are purchasing a wine that they can enjoy at home and confidently serve to friends. Placing all this information in the printed form accompanying a bottle or on the label of wine is an impossible task.

Wine bottle labels are highly valuable spaces. There is wine bottle real estate as well as wine bottle geography. There are areas on the bottle that correspond to areas in the environment. Many wine purchases are made on the spur of the moment. As a result, it is striking how frequently the spatial iconography used on labels is simplistic and frequently naive. A QR Code could provide more information about the region and its identity; it enables a broader branding strategy that combines old and new, tradition and innovation, wine, and technology. Wine labels add a touch of art to the science of wine. QR codes and social media are useful beyond the point of sale. Many different types of wine media can be used to target wine buyers—or to attract new wine buyers. The presence and intervention of QR Codes in wine media is to provide guidance before purchasing wines. The digital versions can be more useful to marketers than the print versions, and there is an entire world of wine online that will never appear printed on paper (Brabazon et al., 2014: 55, 56, 58, 59).

Scanning a QR Code in a retail store is an impulsive, spur-of-the-moment act. The customer wants something, which he (or more likely she) hopes can be obtained by scanning the code, or sees a reason (which the winery, at its best, has written as text next to the code) why he/she should scan the code. Because the scan was most likely impulsive, the information discovered must satisfy the impulse by eliciting a feeling in the person who scanned the code. Give them a monetary reason to smile, such as a coupon or voucher. They would not have scanned the code if they did not already want to buy the wine, so give them a reason to by presenting them excellent reviews from 'experts.' Show them a brief film promising a unique regional taste to tempt them to try something new. Assure them that their friends will be impressed because they have discovered a one-of-a-kind and limited-edition wine that they may not have another opportunity to buy. A YouTube video can be used to explain food pairing and cooking options. Price comparison is one of the most common applications of barcode scanning. A quick scan of a product's barcode (the standard UPC barcode, not a QR Code) can lead a potential customer to websites that will tell them where else they can buy that wine, and, more importantly, where they can buy it for less money. This information is useful to consumers but not to retailers or winemakers. They do not want to assist a customer in finding a cheaper bottle of wine elsewhere. Give the consumer a QR Code (on a label, a neck hanger, or a shelf talker) that they can scan to go directly to a website with information under the producer's control. The QR Code comes second to the printed message. Print publications allow producers and winemakers to reach out to potential customers before they make a purchase decision (Brabazon et al., 2014: 63, 64, 65). Recognized restaurateurs are now including QR Codes on their food menus (for source and nutritional information) and wine lists (for reviews, recommended food pairings and winemaker interviews). Wineries can assist restaurant and bar managers by providing digital QR Code images for this purpose (Brabazon et al., 2014: 68).

QR Codes are best placed on the labels of wine bottles. They are visible when holding the bottle and can be scanned at the point of sale, at home, or in a restaurant. Bottles, like phones, are mobile. According to wineries, the ideal size for a QR Code on a wine bottle label is between 0.5 and 0.8 inches [1.27 cm and 2.03 cm], large enough to be easily scanned but small enough that the scan is not distorted by the bottle's curvature. All information (text, video, audio) linked via a QR Code on a wine bottle label or other collateral material must meet the same compliance standards as claims and information on the label. The wine label's limitations are reduced. As the space encasing the wine expands, so do the possibilities for design innovation. QR Codes are being placed on the front labels of some wineries. In this location, the codes can present a design challenge, but the benefit is that potential customers can see right away that a bottle on a shelf has a QR Code without having to turn the bottle to see the back label. The majority of wineries that use QR Codes on their labels place them on the back. The code can provide detailed information about the wine, its vineyards of origin, the winemaker, aging, recommended foods, and reviews. It can link directly to a webpage (via a URL that can be redirected at any time) or to a menu that allows a person to select the information that he or she wants to see right now—including discount coupons. QR Codes can be etched into bottles, but the cost may be prohibitively high and the quality may be substandard. While a bottle-etched QR Code has cache, including a QR Code on a label rather than the glass itself is likely to be less expensive and easier (Brabazon et al., 2014: 71–73, 75). QR Codes are more than just a one-way communication channel from a winery to a customer. People want to interact. As a result of the use of QR Codes, a customer (or potential customer) can easily call a winery with a question, sign up for a mailing list, join a wine club, or even order wine via m-commerce. Customers can provide feedback on a specific bottle of wine, plan a future wine tour, or inquire about the nearest wine store. With the increasing use of smartphones that support video via Skype, a winery can hold video conversations with customers that are easily launched by a QR Code. This is a great example of immediate personal interaction (Brabazon et al., 2014: 81).

QR Codes in the wine industry include: video tours of the winery; self-guided tours at the winery, with either audio or video recordings at key locations on the tour; QR Codes on back labels that allow customers to learn more about the wine, its source vineyards, the winemaker, recommended foods, and reviews; promotional information, discounts, and specials for smartphone friends of the winery, wine club membership offers, local wine shops, winery forum invitation, wine tastings (Brabazon et al., 2014: 82). Almost all communication media, including brochures, newsletters, tasting sheets, newspapers and magazines, posters and in-winery signage, retail shelves, websites, and food and wine menus, can incorporate and display Codes (Brabazon et al., 2014: 83). The codes are not a marketing campaign in and of themselves, but they can be an important component of any campaign. They serve as the link between the analog and digital worlds (Brabazon et al., 2014: 84).

Table 5.1 The example of the use of *Living Wine Labels* app. Designed by Mojca Ramšak 2021

Step 1	Step 2	Step 3
Download the *Living Wine Labels* app through the Apple App or Google Play Stores. The download of the app is subject to the user being of legal drinking age in their country of use (e.g., checking the age with an imaginative age question to be entered in the application: "Canvasing wine to youngsters isn't one of them. Tell us, friend, what year were you born?").	Scan the label with the phone.	Watch the *Living Wine Label, the experience unfold.*
→	→	

A consumer's information from QR Codes, whether for security or education, is trackable. The data is owned by the brand, and while this information could simply be used to inform marketing decisions, it may be enough to dissuade some privacy-minded wine lovers from participating. For example, an Australian wine brand, "19 Crimes," employs Augmented Reality in its labels. Through its app, one can scan labels, each decorated with different historical convicts exiled to Australia for at least one of 19 crimes that bore such punishment. When you scan the image with the smartphone, the convict's portrait comes to life to recount the tale of banishment. The interactive labels, all accessible from the Living Wine Labels app, include also Napa and Sonoma bottlings from Chateau St. Jean, a range of wines created for the TV show *The Walking Dead* (Teclemariam, 2019), through the stories of women from the past about their trailblazing achievements (e.g., Celia Cruz, freedom singer, 1925–2003, Josephine Baker, show-stopping entertainer and undercover spy, 1906–1975, Nellie Bly, journalist, 1864–1922), learn how to be a Gentleman with tips from Dr. Henry Lindeman, a founder of the Australian wine industry, who started his winery in 1843 and tried to civilize a colony of hard-drinking ruffians by introducing them to more gentlemanly pursuits, and more (Living Wine Labels, 2020). The *Living Wine Labels* app builds on the popularity of the 19 Crimes wine app, which first brought Augmented Reality to wine labels. Table 5.1 shows how to utilize the app Living Wine Labels.

If, for example, the industry wants to addresses an educated and skeptical female population, the images and stories of beautiful film and music icons that exceeded the expectations of their surroundings are used. The aim of this strategy is to encourage women to be determined, bold, and fearless. These icons depicted on wine labels along with their quotes are Josephine Baker, dancer, Nellie Bly, journalist, Celia Cruz, singer. The back of the wine label with these muses also contains their short biographies or "Idea presentations." The wine industry hopes that women will toast in honor of their emancipated predecessors who break through the ceilings above them. The trio of California wines on women is made to empower modern women and to cheer their future and progress when they will do things on their own terms and in their own way. All the labels bring entertainment and engaging experiences to the wine aisle, beginning in February 2018. Similarly, the industry also makes other thematic labels nineteen century's criminals, the British prisoners who were sent to Australia, and now telling us their stories through labels and Augmented Reality. Then there are The Walking Dead thematic labels, the histories of individual wine producers, and so on.

Since then, more and more apps animated the wine or beer labels. For example, in 2018, an app was launched that turns any collection of wine bottles into a multiple-choice blind tasting quiz, inviting players to test their taste buds while learning about wine in a fun and informal environment (Eads, 2018). WineGame was created by two friends after 20 years of conducting low-tech wine tastings with friends. With the help of a software designer, they created a high-tech version, with the game being both entertaining and educational. The way the app works is that a host first enters their wines, taking a photo of each label, before hiding the wine labels from the guests (by wrapping the bottle in tinfoil or bags). All players can log in on their own device using a code generated by the host. The app then generates a multiple-choice quiz in which players must identify the grape, country, region, and vintage/label of wine, in turn, drawing on a database that includes almost every bottle of wine in the world. Three attempts are allowed per question, with points awarded for each level. The technology was used in such a way that all players—from experienced wine drinkers to wine novices—could become winners. WineGame's mission was to replace stigmas about wine education with a fun experience where everyone can experiment, engage with wine, and learn (Eads, 2018).

Similarly, in 2018, beer labels, using Augmented Reality were developed. The Glasgow-based agency designed cans for a local independent brewery using Moby Dick-inspired artistic illustrations. The black and white linocut images had a distinctly nautical theme. They created three designs: Ishmael (American IPA), Yojo (Gose), and Ahab (American Stout). They animated the flat artwork internally to create looping animations, and then created a series of 3D visuals where the packaging literally comes to life on the can. They believe the animated/Augmented Reality possibilities for beverage brands are endless and could help beverage brands better tell their stories of history, process, and provenance (French, 2018).

The growing enthusiasm for multisensory, experiential wine marketing events is being brought to the masses through sensory apps that allow consumers to interact from the comfort of their own homes. All consumers need to do is download the free app from iTunes App Store, scan the back label of their bottle, and then access a carefully curated selection of music tracks (Spence, 2019: 113).

During the 2020 pandemic, an app was developed to allow drinkers to watch a mini virtual dance performance. Consumers start by directly downloading an app or scanning the QR code on a wine product. Then consumers scan a producer and musician's logo on the label to hear a new version of his single and see a 3D animated performance by the group. With each additional product in the frame, more sections of the ad are added until the full song is playable. The app works with interactivity, so the more products in the frame, the more music users hear. Each label scan generates a $1 donation to, among others, American Cancer Society (Hancock, 2020), which is a typical absurdity as permissive commercial alcohol advertising is promoted as "social marketing."

Augmented Reality is an investment and takes time to implement. It does not provide two-way communication, although this is enhanced by gamification. Label scanning can also be problematic with unsafe lighting and operator error. But searching for wine or spirit brand information is clearly demonstrated by the use of phones and their apps in retail stores, restaurants, and tasting rooms (The Wine Industry Advisor, 2019).

In the future, sensory apps and other forms of technological innovation in particular will translate the latest insights around multisensory experiential events into the home environment. Multisensory events go far beyond the traditional wine-tasting format and sell the experience, the multisensory experience, not just the product. Multisensory experiential wine tastings fit into the general framework of the seemingly increasingly popular experience economy and have overtaken products as must-have purchases. It seems increasingly likely that these formats of experiential marketing, seen primarily in the world of wine, are likely to be extended to a range of different alcoholic beverages and from there to a range of different food and drink product categories, as seen from the examples mentioned above (Spence, 2019: 113, 114). As more and more companies offer smart packaging solutions to increase consumer engagement and loyalty and create a direct relationship between producers and their end consumers, this type of fun alcohol purchase is expected to increase (The Wine Industry Advisor, 2019), and at the moment it is not regulated by laws or advertising codes.

(see also the chapter on Digital marketing strategies during a coronavirus pandemic)

References

Alcohol labelling: A discussion document on policy options. (2017). Copenhagen: World health organization regional office for Europe. Retrieved August 24, 2021 from https://www.euro.who.int/__data/assets/pdf_file/0006/343806/WH07_Alcohol_Labelling_full_v3.pdf

Behrens, S., Wiedmann, K.-P., & Hennigs, N. (2013). Wine as luxury experience: A taxonomy of consumers based on best-worst scaling. In K.-P. Wiedmann & N. Hennigs (Eds.), *Luxury marketing: A challenge for theory and practice* (pp. 395–416). Springer Gabler.

Brabazon, T., Winter, M., & Gandy, B. (2014). *Digital wine. How QR codes facilitate new Markets for Small Wine Industries.* Springer Briefs in Business.

Eads, L. (2018, 21 June). New app turns any wine bottle into blind tasting quiz. *The Drinks Business.* Retrieved August 24, 2021 from https://www.thedrinksbusiness.com/2018/06/new-app-turns-any-wine-bottle-into-blind-tasting-quiz/

French, P. (2018, 21 May). Augmented reality beer labels in development. *The Drinks Business.* Retrieved August 24, 2021 from https://www.thedrinksbusiness.com/2018/05/augmented-reality-beer-labels-in-development/

Hancock, E. (2020, 18 September). Black eyed peas create AR music campaign with Barefoot wine. *The Drinks Business.* Retrieved August 24, 2021 from https://www.thedrinksbusiness.com/2020/09/black-eyed-peas-collaborate-on-marketing-stunt-with-barefoot-wine/

Kapferer, J.-N., & Bastien, V. (2009). *The luxury strategy: Break the rules of marketing to build luxury brands.* Philadelphia, Kogan Page.

Living Wine Labels [app on App Store and Google Play]. (2020). Retrieved August 24, 2021 from https://www.livingwinelabels.com/
Michman, R. D., & Mazze, E. M. (2006). *The affluent consumer: Marketing and selling the luxury lifestyle*. Praeger Publishers.
Regulation (EU) No 1151/2012 of European Parliament and of the Council of 21 November 2012 on quality schemes for agricultural products and foodstuffs; Consolidated version (OJ L 343, 14.12.2012, p. 1). Retrieved August 24, 2021 from https://eur-lex.europa.eu/eli/reg/2012/1151/2019-12-14
Spence, C. (2019). Multisensory experiential wine marketing. *Food Quality and Preference, 71*, 106–116. Retrieved August 24, 2021 from https://www.semanticscholar.org/paper/Multisensory-experiential-wine-marketing-Spence/9225828f5db5e8a10f59ab527f07076fa8f52f15
Teclemariam, T. (2019, 5 April). Five Ways Smartphones are Changing How We Drink Wine. *Wine Enthusiast*. Retrieved August 24, 2021 from https://www.winemag.com/2019/04/05/smartphones-wine/
The Wine Industry Advisor. (2019, 21 March). Smart packaging, tech labels, and emerging technology in marketing the wine brand on the bottle. Retrieved August 24, 2021 from https://wineindustryadvisor.com/2019/03/21/smart-packaging-emerging-technology-marketing

Chapter 6
Wearable Technology for Preventive or Curative Purposes

It's a great advantage not to drink among hard drinking people.

F. Scott Fitzgerald, The Great Gatsby

Abstract The prospects of wearable technology as purpose-built wearables for preventive or curative reasons are discussed in this chapter, as well as how they can assist lessen the burden of alcoholism as a chronic disease. A better assessment of the situation in terms of monitoring and prevention is feasible by integrating various technical advances with traditional methodologies. Positive technologies also help to minimize the cultural stigma associated with alcoholism. Although technological advancements and availability may assist people who are addicted to or consume dangerous amounts of alcohol, there are still numerous obstacles to overcome, including ethical, legal, and the most significant issue of keeping up with the alcohol industry, which is far more evolved than alcoholism prevention.

In healthcare, wearable technologies are defined as noninvasive and autonomous devices that collect, analyze, and aggregate physiological data to improve personal health and well-being (Balfe et al., 2019: 2). Wearable technologies have been used almost exclusively for fitness purposes, driven by the growing need for consumers to monitor their own health. The integration of wearable tech (e.g., hearables, smartwatches, fitness trackers, eyewear, body devices, and skin patches) with Augmented Reality (AR), Big Data, Artificial Intelligence, and cloud computing solutions, as well as the decreasing prices of sensors, open-source application programming interfaces (APIs), frameworks and libraries, are enabling faster and more cost-effective solutions within the Internet of Things (IoT) ecosystem. Recent advances are adding value to healthcare with a focus on diagnosis, treatment, monitoring, and prevention. These benefits are being felt across the healthcare chain, with benefits such as personalization, early diagnosis, remote patient monitoring (RPM), medication adherence, information libraries, and better decision-

M. Ramšak, *Social Impact of Wine Marketing*, Contributions to Management Science, https://doi.org/10.1007/978-3-030-89224-1_6

making while reducing healthcare costs. Moreover, the growing demand and functionality have drawn the attention of insurers and enterprises to provide wearable health technology to consumers and employees due to its far-reaching benefits (Balfe et al., 2019: 2).

In the field of alcoholism prevention, health programs using mobile apps to prevent drinking, reduce drinking, or achieve complete sobriety[1] are designed for alcoholics and not preventive, i.e., before the onset of alcoholism. Curative alcoholism interventions and treatments, on the other hand, use new technologies to collect data on how, where, and under what conditions people drink alcohol.

With the help of technology, researchers can more accurately measure, record, and track alcohol-related drinking habits. The data obtained in this way are more reliable than traditional self-reporting (Makarić, 2018). Combining different technological achievements makes it possible to assess the situation at the time of the event. Thus, different reporting logs (on the phone or computer) in conjunction with a GPS location and a mobile phone that collects data on current movement and drinking alcohol, and sensors capable of measuring current blood alcohol content can provide a wealth of data (stress, impact, motivation to drink, craving for alcohol, environmental, and contextual factors) about what happens before, during and after alcohol use. Alcohol-related drinking habits data obtained with the help of technology help to investigate the factors associated with different patterns of behavior and prevent the negative consequences of alcohol use in adults as well as in adolescents (Makarić, 2018).

An example of a mobile app aimed at developing low-risk drinking habits in young adults is Boozebuster (Boumparis et al., 2021), which focuses on the importance of motivation, self-efficacy, and environmental constraints on drinking. Behavior change techniques used include personalized normative feedback, motivational interviewing, cognitive-behavioral therapy, goal setting, self-monitoring, protective behavioral strategies, and mindfulness. Boozebuster consists of a total of seven modules and was developed with the following rationale: The personalized normative feedback module serves as an initial assessment of young adult drinking behavior and compares it to peer norms and official drinking guidelines. This process creates awareness among individuals of their drinking compared to peers and has been shown to be an effective approach for initiating change related to drinking. The integrated motivational interviewing module motivates individuals to change their alcohol-related behaviors by helping them build confidence in their ability to achieve their goals. In addition, Boozebuster includes a number of lifestyle support modules, such as relaxation, sleep improvement, drinking diary, gratitude diary, and an emergency button specifically designed to provide recommendations

[1] Quit drinking apps, such as Quit Drinking—Stay Sober, Sober Time, Sober Grid, Sobriety Tracker, Twenty-Four Hours a Day, Sobriety Counter, Sober Tool, No More!, Nomo, AlcoDroid Achocol Tracker, I am Sober, Dry Days by AlcoChange, Alcohol Addiction Calendar, Stop Drinking with Andrew Johnson, Happify, Coach.me, 12 Steps AA Companion, Self Hypnosis to Stop Drinking... In July 2020, androids could access over a hundred of these apps in English.

for acute cravings. These modules give individuals tools to manage cravings, peer pressure, and stress that might otherwise interfere with their alcohol consumption goals. Providing young adults with a mobile app that promotes low-risk drinking habits while providing lifestyle-related support components may be a promising approach to increase the reach, acceptability, and effectiveness of behavior change interventions aimed at reducing alcohol use in this population (Boumparis et al., 2021).

A variety of sensors that measure blood alcohol content and are convenient and easy to use are also helpful in measuring. In the treatment of alcohol addiction, there has been a need to combine traditional methods with new technology. In support of traditional treatment, screening tests, forms, and schedules are now available in electronic form that can facilitate entry into the treatment process itself. Electronic behavioral-cognitive therapy and other supportive applications are available that improve outpatient care by standardizing some parts of therapy or even creating a complete treatment protocol. With the help of technology, treatment is no longer tied only to outpatient care, but patients have access to various strategies, support, information, etc. also from home, so they have the option of ongoing care. Such technology is helpful for people with fewer problems due to alcohol consumption, while there is less evidence of efficacy in people who have more problems or are addicted to alcohol (Makarić, 2018).

Perceived social stigma and high costs may discourage people from seeking professional help. Mobile phones have gained acceptance in almost all strata of society and promise to be a ubiquitous treatment platform through which there is a constant digital connection between the user and the application. These applications are typically a less costly alternative to face-to-face treatment approaches. The use of positive technology, a term that refers to the use of mobile technologies to promote self-determination and improve the quality of life and emotional well-being of patients, is emerging as a promising complement to traditional treatment. The format and content of mobile phone applications range from simple text-based approaches to interactive interventions that can be used in a hybrid format or even as a standalone approach in the treatment of mental health problems. In addition to lower costs, reduced stigma, and increased convenience for patients and healthcare providers, the appeal of smartphone applications lies in their ability to capture user data throughout the day and provide ongoing coaching (Seçkin, 2016: 45).

While alcohol locks or blocking devices, which require the alcohol content of the driver's exhaled air not to exceed a certain limit as a condition for starting a car, have a long history in the United States, this practice is slowly being introduced in Europe. To date, several EU countries (Sweden, Finland, Poland, Denmark, the Netherlands, Belgium, France, and Austria) have introduced compulsory installation of alcohol locks as part of rehabilitation programs in the case of driving under the influence of alcohol, and Lithuania, Luxembourg, and Ireland are already in the process of introduction (Makarić, 2018).

With the development of technology, helping people with risky and harmful alcohol consumption or addiction has become available to a wider audience. Often such people do not have the opportunity to visit help centers or the aid is financially unaffordable for them. For example, when dealing with people with less drinking problems, an application can be used that primarily informs the person about the problem and the sources of help. There are also apps that, in addition to sources of help, offer alcohol withdrawal strategies and guide the individual through the entire process. With sensors that can be built into a bracelet or other handy device, as well as breathalyzer and mobile apps, an individual can monitor their drinking habits and current intake, which can deter them from dangerous behavior and prevent the harmful effects of alcohol use. The advantage of technological advances is also that they provide the desired data and information systematically and immediately. When the desire for alcohol arises, the bracelet immediately warns when the amount of alcohol consumed has exceeded the limit. If the desire persists, one can help himself with one of the strategies that distract from doing so. At the same time, one can immediately write down feelings and thoughts in a diary on the smartphone. All this is fed and recorded and helps the individual to become aware of his/her habits and can encourage him to take action (Makarić, 2018).

It is important to emphasize, however, that technological advances also bring many new challenges and ethical dilemmas. Some devices used for research purposes may collect so much data that there is a need for a new technology that will be able to properly analyze and use all this data. When observing alcohol-related drinking habits, people can change their behavior because they know they are being observed, or they are not following a research protocol. The data obtained in these circumstances are therefore not necessarily correct and may lead researchers to erroneous conclusions. Technology can also fail, break down, and transmit missing or incorrect data at any time. An ethical issue also remains open, and researchers are still working on how to protect personal data and maintain the confidentiality of user data. There are more and more gadgets and devices on the market, apps that are not supported by research that would confirm the reliability and effectiveness, or this research is still ongoing when the product can already be purchased and used. Therefore, much research is needed to confirm the accuracy and timeliness of data presentation of all new technologies for detecting alcohol in the blood or exhaled air and the effectiveness of new technological approaches to presenting strategies in the treatment of alcohol addiction (Makarić, 2018).

References

Boumparis, N., Schulte, M. H., Kleiboer, A., Huizink, A., & Riper, H. (2021) A mobile intervention to promote low-risk drinking habits in young adults: Protocol for a randomized controlled trial. *JMIR Research Protocols* 10 (6) Retrieved August 24, 2021 from https://www.researchprotocols.org/2021/6/e29750

Makarić, S. (2018, 13 September). Tehnologija v svetu alkohola. *MOSA*. Retrieved August 24, 2021 from http://www.infomosa.si/clanki/tehnologija-v-svetu-alkohola.html

Seçkin, G. (2016). Digitized emotions in the pocket: Social computing and Mobile mental health (mMH) applications. In Y. Sharon, S. Y. Tettegah, & Y. E. Garcia (Eds.), *Emotions, technology, and health* (pp. 41–62). Elsevier.

Balfe, R., Young, A., Jakimaviciute, U., Bain, B., Undisclosed (London, UK), Undisclosed (Guildford, Uk) (2019, August). *Wearable technology in healthcare. Report GDHCHT026*. GlobalData. Retrieved August 24, 2021 from https://www.tauli.cat/institut/wp-content/uploads/2020/06/wearables-GlobalData_WearableTechnologyinHealthcare_220819.pdf

Chapter 7
Children and Adolescents as a Marketing Target

But in college, we can wear our alcohol abuse as proudly as our university sweatshirts; the two concepts are virtually synonymous.

Koren Zailckas, Smashed: Story of a Drunken Girlhood

Abstract Because no one can legally or by self-regulation manage this gray area, the options for marketing alcohol to children and teenagers are essentially limitless. As a result, this chapter focuses on some of the strategies employed by the alcohol business to convert young people into lifelong drinkers, including the use of modern technology. Marketers purposefully target teenagers, especially first-time drinkers, novice drinkers, and rebels, with alcohol. They are experts at market segmentation, taking into account demographic, regional, and psychological characteristics. It goes without saying that the development of lifelong drinkers begins at a young age, and that the contest for their attention is unfair and full of deception. The types of alcoholic drinks that young people enjoy change all the time, and new drinks, packaging, or sensory stimulation are promoted through marketing that targets young people specifically.

The alcohol industry perfectly maintains the visibility of its brands in a situation of advertising ban. The industry knows how to look for opportunities in nonalcoholic products and services that can be used to communicate with consumers. It is obvious that the creation of lifelong drinkers starts early and that the fight for them is unfair and with all the tricks. Children are potential future targets for the alcohol industry, and alcohol marketers are making sure they keep up with the times and create a universally accepted way of drinking for all. They are excellent at market fragmentation and take into account demographic, geographic, and psychological variables. If they want to attract women, they stereotypically go for glamour and appeal to women in a way that makes them feel admired. When they want to capture the male imagination, they stereotypically prioritize masculinity and sport victories, which in many cultures includes alcohol. Because alcohol is socially acceptable, they

M. Ramšak, *Social Impact of Wine Marketing*, Contributions to Management Science, https://doi.org/10.1007/978-3-030-89224-1_7

systematically introduce it to the youth market, among first tasters, novice drinkers, and rebels who, along with cigarettes and first sexual intercourse, drink alcohol as initiation into the adult world.

Bans on alcohol advertising do not deter alcohol marketers even if they want to offer alcohol indirectly to children. Children are slowly introduced to the acceptability of drinking with the help of alcohol candies and even more so with colorful flavored alcoholic beverages "alcopops" with relatively low alcohol content (e.g., 3–7% alcohol by volume or stronger, which are premixed spirits and often contain about 12.5% alcohol by volume). The group of alcopops drinks consists of three types: malt beverages to which various fruit juices or other flavorings have been added, wine-based beverages to which ingredients such as fruit juice or other flavorings have been added (wine coolers), and beverages containing distilled alcohol and sweet liquids such as fruit juices or other flavorings. Other names for alcopops include flavored malt beverage, pre-packaged spirit or premium packaged spirit, and ready-to-drink (Alcopop 2021). Then there are sweets containing alcohol, that is, those with liquor, "which are not for children," but which children eat secretly when they meet them, and chocolates and larger imitation chocolates wrapped in glittering foil, simulating the shape of champagne bottles. They may appear cheap, but they build children's tolerance for drinking and satisfy their drive to imitate adults since they create a lasting effect on them. They're tools for disguising drinking as an attractive habit.

Observations from the Health Behaviour in School-aged Children and World Health Organization collaborative cross-national study (Vieno et al., 2018: 38) suggest that the types of alcoholic beverages that adolescents consume are constantly changing and new beverages, such as alcopops in the late 1990s, are promoted through marketing that particularly appeals to young people. The consumption of alcopops from 2006 onward, after it became clear that these drinks were gaining popularity with young people, concerns grew about their appeal, particularly to underage drinkers. Interestingly, since the introduction of a question on alcopops in the international research Health Behaviour in School-Aged Children in 2006, the average prevalence of weekly consumption has fallen from 11% to 5%, contradicting the idea that alcopops were becoming a substitute for spirits and would be associated with riskier drinking patterns. The highest levels of weekly alcopops consumption were among girls in Ireland/UK in 2006 (20%), but this has since fallen to 3%, consistent with other European sub-regions (Vieno et al., 2018: 38).

The prevalence of weekly use of alcopops was below 5% among girls in 24 countries and regions in 2014, and among boys in 21. Among girls, the highest prevalence of alcopop use was observed in Malta (14%) and Denmark (10%), and the lowest in Finland, Iceland, Ireland, Portugal, Russian Federation, and Slovakia (all 1%). The highest prevalence among boys was found in Malta (16%) and Denmark and Israel (11%), and the lowest in Iceland, Ireland, and Norway (2%). There was a significant gender difference in 14 countries and regions, with higher consumption among boys. Weekly consumption of alcopops has also declined since 2006 in many countries and regions, with overall prevalence falling from 11% to 4%

among girls and from 11% to 5% among boys. The largest decreases were observed among girls in England, Wales, Ukraine, Scotland, and Austria, where prevalence was highest in 2006 (Pavlova & Inchle, 2018: 14–15).

The Danish advertiser and the globe's foremost marketing expert Martin Lindstrom warned about manipulations in alcohol industry by asking a simple question: "How do you create a lifelong drinker? Start him or her off early by rolling out sweet, flavored, colored, soda-like beverages (laden with alcohol), 'alcopops'". Though they are allegedly intended to be consumed by adults, an American Medical Association study found that alcopops are most popular among thirteen-year-old girls and that these kid-friendly, candylike cocktails make up 29% of the alcohol this group consumes" (Lindstrom, 2011: 29). Besides, the market also offers nonalcoholic beverages for children, especially in the pre-holiday weeks, that mimic the characteristics of alcoholic beverages, e.g., champagne and cocktails and thus inadvertently prepare them for drinking alcoholic mixtures in later years.

Bubble drinks are grateful market drink. Indeed, they are often featured in advertisements for children that contain a plethora of visual metaphors, visual representations of ideas, and verbal metaphors. Because the boundaries between visual and verbal metaphors are not clear and are highly contextual, they can also be heavily abused. Visual metaphors are easily used to encourage children to drink alcohol, even if the advertisements do not promote it at all. In the free baking catalogs before the New Year, we find recipes for "children's champagne," a homemade mixture of apple juice and mineral water, served in a small champagne glass. The symbolism is obvious: children who are supposed to drink this drink do not call it juice with mineral water, but get used to calling it Kinderersekt. The terrain for further alcohol consumption is staked out, because the goal of this marketing of Kinderersekt is to appropriate the festive moment so that other brands of nonalcoholic beverages will not come close later. The moment a child drinks children's sparkling wine will be remembered by them and the account of that memory will later be marketed to them by the adult sparkling wine industry.

Such advertisements for children's sparkling wine are, in a visual sense, a special form of alcohol guerrilla marketing and a tactic known as "Farmgate." Lindstrom explains industry parlance that "marketers use the term 'Farmgate' to refer to the strategy of planting a (false) image of a real, all-natural working farm in our minds, and 'Factorygate' to refer to the fact that most everything we see before us is actually manufactured by a large corporation" (Lindstrom, 2011: 52). "Farmgate" tactic advertises alcohol in dewy jars and bottles as if it had just come from some cold cellar. It is a proven sensory tactic for advertising freshness and cleanliness that hints at the symbolism of unspoiled nature and bioprocessing with unconscious drip symbolism. Some companies even have a precisely calculated number of bubbles or drops that may appear on their glasses in advertisements, as they know their market well and know what arouses a strong desire in consumers to buy. They have measured the best specific intensity of murmur and bubbling of drinks when poured into glasses (Lindstrom, 2011: 52–56, 65–66), specific color shades of alcohol that appear in ads and can attract young people.

"The truth is," Lindstrom comments, "no matter how much we believe we're in control, when it comes to craving, we are often powerless in the face of these triggers. Companies know this, which is why they deliberately imbue their packaging and advertising with 'unconscious signals'—cues that lie just beneath our conscious awareness, right at those moments when cravings are liable to strike. At Coca-Cola, for example, marketing executives spend hours discussing how many bubbles they should feature in their print ads and on in-store refrigerators. Realizing how much craving bubbles generate—they make us think of that cool, refreshing feeling of carbonation hitting our palates—some executives have actually come up with a confidential model for how many bubbles they need to trigger our cravings" (Lindstrom, 2011: 65).

Ambitious alcohol marketers, of course, do not just market certain moments, but entire periods. A convincing method for selling nostalgia is to use a verbal or visual metaphor to mention time, because what we buy is frequently not simply a product, but a concept that that object symbolizes (e.g., health, happiness, sightseeing, purity, spirituality, etc.). Especially in the pre-New Year period, retailers offer many products that combine a seeming tradition with new imaginary needs. Thus, in October, they start selling Advent calendars for adults of both sexes, which offer cosmetics, sweet treats, snacks, drinks such as champagne, boutique wines, gin, beer, whiskey, tea, or cigars. In the Advent calendars that appeared in the Anglo-American world at the beginning of the 20th century and in which there were initially only short biblical records, after the Second World War, there were also chocolates for children, and later, new products were added, e.g., toys and crayons. The industry of all kinds has also found a niche market for the sale of adult products in Advent calendars. The characteristic of such a form of sale, including alcohol, is the deliberate infantilization of young adult women and the emphasis on a dazzling lifestyle, which is a substitute for the actual lack of social power of women. Once the alcohol industry achieves the childishness of adult behavior, when they are distracted by advertisements, and when the industry convinces them that naivety is the normal behavior of an adult woman, it also easily sells them Advent calendars. By reeducating and selling to noncritical customers, the alcohol industry is slowly enforcing the normalization of alcohol consumption, which denies all the harmful consequences of alcohol consumption. These, however, do not only cause damage to the body due to alcoholism but also accidents and violence due to it, children born with alcohol syndrome, male impotence, and sexually transmitted diseases due to daring alcoholic promiscuity.

This already brings us to a new artifice of alcohol marketing, the creation of special effects that co-create a multisensory shopping and drinking experience (Mclennan, 2016). These include ready-made hybrid drinks (mixes of alcohol and nonalcoholic drinks and mixes of several types of alcohol) in packaging for one person, color-changing alcohol when mixed with other drinks (e.g., black gin and tonic that turns purple when mixed). Besides, there are also those in this category whose preparation is dangerous, such as burning or smoking beverages and beverages prepared with dry ice. These drinks with special effects that stimulate the senses (e.g., that are interesting to look at, have unusual ingredients, a strange taste or, conversely, are odorless, but contain tannins that dry out the oral mucosa, resulting in more saliva, which intensifies the taste, with the method of preparation, with drinking glasses with an unusual surface and with the method of drinking, such as a vapor-shaped drink that you inhale), give the impression of the drama with which young people want to put themselves in front of their peers. Multisensory drinking is also marketed on certain holidays, Halloween is such an example, when alcoholic cocktails with "body parts" are popular, for instance, with frozen palms, fruity eyes, and a bloodred color. The market trend of multisensory offers the alcohol industry the opportunity to include drinking-fun adventures with an alchemy of different scents and visual and hearing effects, and another exciting choice of drinking alcohol in addition to standard drinking norms in an alcohol-saturated market. Multisensory drinking is an interactive and mesmerizing experience for the consumer, a good joke to put yourself in front of others and can be found on the Internet in no time. As multisensory drinking with special effects is currently on the rise, some universities have special departments for their research and marketing.

In recent years, the more traditional approaches to sensory marketing have increasingly been complemented by technology-driven interventions, often inspired by the outcomes of multisensory experiential events (Spence, 2019: 113).

For example, the experience of tasting wine can sometimes change dramatically for consumers simply by changing the music they listen to (Spence, 2019). After the first decade of the 21st century, there was an explosion of interest in multisensory experiential events in the wine, whiskey, beer, vodka, or other spirits industry. There were not just alcohol-music experiences (for adults), but all kinds of multisensory tasting events. In many cases, recordings of wineries and cellars from around the world were transformed into soundscapes that could be listened to while enjoying the wines, or, as the opposite experience, tastings of wines in silence or with background noise as well as occasional sounds that could distract the taster's attention. Visual cues, such as color and lighting or other visual stimuli, such as projections on the wall, and tactile aspects of multisensory wine tastings are also important; for example, tasters prefer wine significantly more under red lighting and listening to sweet music than under all other conditions, or looking at a smiling face may improve ratings of the sweetness of an unfamiliar juice blend compared to the rating received when looking at an angry/upset face instead. The multisensory experience could also influence wine selection in a supermarket or wine store. For example, classical music might lead customers to buy more expensive wine rather than just more wine per se; or the majority of customers might buy French wine when French music is playing in the background, while buying more German wine when German music is playing over the speakers. The recommendation of what music to use is based on demographic factors, e.g., blues and classic rock might appeal more to younger people (Spence, 2019: 107, 108, 112, 113).

Targeting, appealing, and attracting people with children in wine market segments is also part of a latent wine tourism. Studies show the destination-level constraints about the lack of activities and a destination image that is friendly to children. People with children are attracted to places where there are many options to "occupy" and edutain their children. Collaborative efforts in tourism and not tourism firms (e.g., transportation companies, restaurants museums, leisure centers, and schools) customize the infrastructure to make it accessible and attractive to this dormant market niche, and subsequently, promote the region and destination as a children-friendly destination. The study on the factors motivating as well as inhibiting people with children to (re)-visit wineries in Adelaide, Australia (Sigala, 2019), shows that the residents were more concerned about the social stigma to them involving or taking their children to wineries than tourists. Instead, tourists gave more emphasis on concerns related to infrastructure and services that may be available to cater for their children's needs. This is not surprising because nobody knows and can recognize the tourists in a foreign country and tourists may also not care what local people say or may think about them taking their children to wineries. Both, the local people and the tourist have the interest and willingness to experience and enjoy wine tourism experiences after having children. Thus, it is important how wineries develop and adopt strategies that focus on maintaining relations with their customers throughout their whole lifecycle and do not lose opportunities from this latent demand (Sigala, 2019: 111, 120).

The younger a consumer who starts using a product or brand, the more likely they are to use it for life. Of course, the feedback loop on the influence of parents' drinking habits, which shape lifelong preferences, is not insignificant. Through the characters of wine queens and the exposure of the sophisticated wine drinking that they promote, the alcohol industry also effectively markets our fear of failure, loneliness, loss of control over our own lives, glorifies leisure, and plays the card of affiliation. In this way, the image of a successful person is anchored. Success is understood as a social person who attends various events and likes to socialize with other people (preferably with a glass of wine in his/her hand) and sets himself/herself up to a photojournalist to be "immortalized" forever in the gossip magazine columns. If photographers are not nearby, selfies and posts on social networks are also working fine.

Some cultural events also targeting younger audiences, e.g., film festivals that have accompanying wine programs and are conceptually part of these events. These events maintain and gain new wine customers and their loyalty through an experiential economy that connects business with unusual and memorable experiences (Dolan, 2018). And young people are the population that not only buys goods or services but products with an active, authentic experience or with similar added value for which they are willing to give money.

Alcohol advertising at sporting events is also an important potential advertising medium for children. Alcohol content displayed on TV, including alcohol advertising and branding, is known to influence adolescent alcohol intake (Barker et al., 2020: 1, 6). A 2018 study (Barker et al., 2020) of United Kingdom population exposure to alcohol content, including branding, in United Kingdom broadcasts of the 2018 Formula 1 Championship showed that audio-visual alcohol content, including branding and in particular Heineken and Johnnie Walker branding, was highly prevalent in the broadcast footage of the 2018 Formula 1 Championship races and that the total amount of alcohol content was greater in 2018 than in 2017. The alcohol content in the broadcast race footage generated significant population exposure and delivered billions of viewer impressions. This included more than 100 million gross impressions of branded alcohol among children under 16. Alcohol content was prevalent at all races, even races held in countries with alcohol advertising restrictions. Alcohol advertising through sponsorship during these events appears to be changing with the inclusion of computer-generated alcohol advertising introduced in the 2018 Championship. As the Formula 1 Championships are international events with global audiences, the population exposure figures on the United Kingdom are likely to represent a very small proportion of the true global total exposure. Some alcohol producers linked their advertising to messages about responsible consumption. Heineken, for example, linked its five-year Formula 1 sponsorship to a significant cause of preventable physical, mental and social harm, and in particular to one of the leading causes of death on our roads, drink-driving. This global campaign included Heineken's signature red star and green branding on billboards that also carry a prominent "When You Drive, Never Drink" message. Heineken has stated that it will use Formula 1 to promote this campaign and the Heineken 0.0 brand. The Heineken 0.0 ad could act as an alibi for alcoholic products, not least because it uses the same brand imagery (a star in Heineken's case) on alcoholic and nonalcoholic products, so potential consumers, particularly young people, may not be able to distinguish between advertising for alcoholic and nonalcoholic Heineken products. This industry tactic could potentially serve a subtle public relations function by generating goodwill among potential consumers of the brand while increasing advertising for its alcoholic products, thereby promoting brand preference and product consumption. In addition, the proportion of Heineken 0.0 advertising has decreased significantly since 2017, with 2017 Heineken 0.0 posters being replaced by regular Heineken posters. The majority of Formula 1 Championship races (18 out of 21) aired on a Sunday before 9 pm—a time when children are likely to be watching what their parents are watching. The Formula 1 Championship footage broadcast gave children millions of impressions of branded alcohol and breached the Office's Code of Communications Broadcasting, which states that "before the watershed ... the misuse of alcohol must never be condoned, encouraged or glamorized and scenes showing such material should generally be avoided unless there is editorial justification." All Formula 1 races featured scenes of drivers celebrating their victory by drinking from and splashing from champagne bottles, a traditional celebration in Formula 1, which could potentially associate driving with alcohol consumption and glorify alcohol consumption by showing drivers drinking alcohol. Alcohol advertising appeared in United Kingdom broadcast footage of races in countries where alcohol advertising is banned, such as Russia, France, and Bahrain, raising concerns that alcohol brands are circumventing country-specific regulations at Formula 1 races. Race footage with billboard advertising has also been broadcast around the world, which could circumvent alcohol advertising regulations for advertising at sports venues (Barker et al., 2020: 1, 4, 6).

Sports broadcasts also have the highest number of alcohol ads of any TV programming genre in the United States. More than half of all beer advertising on television occurs during the broadcast of sporting events. Alcohol has become a hallmark of game day, not only because fans drink in stadiums and at food stands, but also because alcohol-related commercials dominate the broadcast. American viewers spend about three hours watching football every Sunday, only to see about 11 minutes of the actual game. The rest of the program consists of 20 commercial breaks with about 100 different commercials, most of which are alcohol-related. While this may not seem problematic to some, the product placement is very concerning due to the fact that children are exposed to these messages. Advertisements shown during sports broadcasts are subject to different regulations than what may be shown on television, which means that children of all ages are exposed to alcohol-related advertising messages that they would not otherwise see (Hilliard, 2021).

References

Alcopop. (2021). *Wikipedia* Retrieved August 24, 2021 https://en.wikipedia.org/wiki/Alcopop

Barker, A., Opazo-Breton, M., Thomson, E., Britton, J., Grant-Braham, B., & Murray, R. L. (2020). Quantifying alcohol audio-visual content in UK broadcasts of the 2018 Formula 1 Championship: A content analysis and population exposure. *BMJ Open* Retrieved August 24, 2021 from https://bmjopen.bmj.com/content/10/8/e037035

Dolan, D. (2018, 7 February). Engaging consumers with digital tools in today's experience economy. *Wine Industry Advisor.* Retrieved August 24, 2021 from https://wineindustryadvisor.com/2018/02/07/engaging-consumers-digital-experience-economy

Hilliard, J. (2021, 22 June). Alcohol in TV. *Alcohol Rehab Guide.* Retrieved August 24, 2021 from https://www.alcoholrehabguide.org/alcohol/alcohol-in-popular-culture/tv/

Lindstrom, M. (2011). *Brandwashed: Tricks companies use to manipulate our minds and persuade us to buy.* Crown Business.

Mclennan, E. (2016, 22 December). *Top trends in alcoholic drinks.* Retrieved August 24, 2021 from https://www.drinks-insight-network.com/features/featuretop-trends-in-alcoholic-drinks-5724974/w

Pavlova, D., & Inchle, J. (2018). Trends in consumption of different types of alcoholic drink, by gender and subregion. In J. Inchley, D. Currie, A. Vieno, T. Torsheim, C. Ferreira-Borges, M. M. Weber, V. Barnekow, & J. Breda (Eds.), *Adolescent alcohol-related behaviours: Trends and inequalities in the WHO European region, 2002–2014. Observations from the health behaviour in school-aged children (HBSC) WHO collaborative cross-national study* (pp. 13–18). World Health Organization.

Sigala, M. (2019). Wine tourists with children: A constrained-based approach for Untapping a latent wine tourism market segment. In M. Sigala & R. N. S. Robinson (Eds.), *Management and Marketing of Wine Tourism Business: Theory, practice, and cases* (pp. 101–126). Palgrave Macmillan.

Spence, C. (2019). Multisensory experiential wine marketing. *Food Quality and Preference, 71*, 106–116. Retrieved August 24, 2021 from https://www.semanticscholar.org/paper/Multisensory-experiential-wine-marketing-Spence/9225828f5db5e8a10f59ab527f07076fa8f52f15

Vieno, A., Inchley, J., & Currie, D. (2018). Discusssion and conclusion. In J. Inchley, D. Currie, A. Vieno, T. Torsheim, C. Ferreira-Borges, M. M. Weber, V. Barnekow, & J. Breda (Eds.), *Adolescent alcohol-related behaviours: Trends and inequalities in the WHO European region, 2002–2014. Observations from the health behaviour in school-aged children (HBSC) WHO collaborative cross-national study* (pp. 37–43). World Health Organization.

Chapter 8
Social Media, Alcohol, and Young People

"What is this place?"
"Heaven." She laughed, "with better drinks!"

Tan Redding, A Banquet of Crumbs

Abstract This chapter discusses the social and health repercussions of young people being exposed to alcohol marketing on a frequent and indefinite basis through alcohol-related advertising on social media. Adolescents are most commonly exposed to alcohol usage in a positive context on social media, and they are more susceptible to the intoxicating effects of alcohol due to their physical immaturity and lower tolerance levels. Adolescent alcohol use is connected to a higher risk of self-harm and suicide attempts, which has a negative influence on mental health. Social networking platforms are extremely important for young people in maintaining both real-life and virtual friendships. Warnings from credible institutions reach only a small number of people in a way that would change the situation. When it comes to alcohol advertising to young people and in general, social media is a poorly regulated bottomless pit. Young people's behavior, which tends toward "social liking," is influenced by social norms and peer pressure.

According to the World Health Organization alcohol is an age-restricted toxic substance associated with over 200 health conditions, diseases, and injuries (Alcohol Factsheet, 2015). Adolescents are more vulnerable to the intoxicating effects of alcohol due to their physical immaturity and lower tolerance levels, and alcohol use in adolescence adversely affects mental health as it is associated with a higher risk of self-harm and suicide attempts. Adolescent alcohol use also poses risks to long-term health and well-being, both by impairing important brain development processes and by establishing drinking patterns that persist into adulthood. For example, early initiation of alcohol use is associated with an increased likelihood of developing alcohol abuse or dependence in adolescence and adulthood, as well as dependence at a younger age (Briefing 2019). Nevertheless, young people are regularly exposed to

M. Ramšak, *Social Impact of Wine Marketing*, Contributions to Management Science, https://doi.org/10.1007/978-3-030-89224-1_8

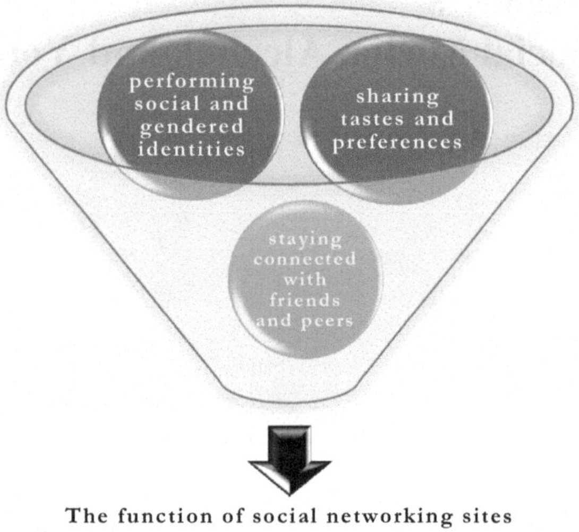

Fig. 8.1 The function of social networking sites in connection to the consumption of alcohol. Source: Designed by Mojca Ramšak 2021

alcohol marketing, including in print media, on television, in alcohol advertising in public spaces at sporting, music and cultural events, and in social media, which changes their drinking behavior and attitudes.

Social networking sites in particular have become ubiquitous in our everyday lives and influence how we interact with each other. For young people, social networking sites are particularly important for maintaining friendships in the real sense as well as online friends. The ability to post photos, make comments, organize nights out and relive them the next day is an essential part of these relationships. Many of the photos tell visual stories and with accompanying text, young people construct identities in specific ways (Lindsay & Supski, 2017: 55) (Fig. 8.1 depicts the role of social networking sites in relation to alcohol use.). Although there are many social networking sites such as Instagram, Twitter, and Pinterest, as well as MySpace and Bebo, and country-specific sites such as StudiVZ (in Germany), the majority of research on young people and alcohol has focused on Facebook, the predominant global social networking site, and has used self-reports of alcohol-related displays on social networks (Lindsay & Supski, 2017: 55; Litt et al., 2018). Alcohol-related tweets are also prevalent among young adults, and the proportion of one's tweets that relate to alcohol is significantly associated with willingness to drink, alcohol use, and negative consequences (Litt et al., 2018). Alcohol-related social media posts (alcoposts) by adolescents' act through user correlates. Positive associations with alcohol use are more visible than negative ones and are typically placed on participants' timelines by others (through the function of tagging). Alcoposts tend to receive more likes and comments than other posts. Such social media grammar likely leads to a normalization of drinking and a tendency to underestimate alcohol-related risks among adolescents and young adults (WHO, 2020: 2).

Alcohol-related social norms are related to the use of social media and television, which promote positive social norms toward alcohol use and subsequently increase adolescent drinking behavior. On social media, adolescents encounter numerous positive alcohol messages communicated by their own close friends and peers. These positive messages have a positive influence on adolescents' alcohol-related social norms. Social norms have a noticeable influence on behavior. Social norms that promote alcohol use are associated with increased alcohol consumption. People's behavior is shaped by observing the behavior of their peers. On social media, adolescents can observe the behavior and communication of a variety of peers by viewing posted photos, texts, and other communications. On social media, adolescents are most often exposed to alcohol use in a positive context (toward alcohol consumption). This exposure could have a positive influence on alcohol-related social norms and thus on drinking behavior. Thus, powerful social norms can be created via social media, and these norms can influence adolescents' drinking behavior (Boers et al., 2020: 1, 4). Posting alcohol-related content is not only a direct reflection of the sharer's alcohol consumption, but may also be a reflection of alcohol-related social cognitions (i.e., perceived norms and attitudes) that are known to predict alcohol consumption. Older adolescents' heavy episodic drinking behavior during the previous year predicted the frequency with which they posted alcohol references on social networking sites, and frequent posting of alcohol use content on social networking sites predicted later alcohol use. There is an association between alcohol-related cognitions and alcohol postings on social media. Alcohol-related postings on social networking sites are common among young adults, and these postings are associated with future problematic alcohol use or vice versa (Litt et al., 2018).

There is also a correlation between young people's frequent exposure to online alcohol marketing with binge drinking, as well as with the likelihood of starting to drink in the first place (WHO, 2020: 2–3). Of particular importance is the impact of alcohol marketing on young people's drinking behavior. The sophistication of alcohol marketing operates implicitly and explicitly. Explicitly, young people trust the industry-mediated knowledge and messages presented in key areas of youth culture, and are critically reflexive readers of the alcohol and alcohol marketing environments in which they operate (which includes the online environment). Implicitly, young people are so immersed in the intoxigenic social environment that alcohol marketing is under the radar and taken for granted. Taking the availability and presence of alcohol for granted leads to a normalization of alcohol consumption by young people in everyday life (Lindsay & Supski, 2017: 51).

Pro-drinking comments on social media can increase both the desire to drink and engagement in advertising, and both can be predictive of future drinking behavior (WHO, 2020: 5). Viewing alcohol ads on social media is significantly associated with increased risky drinking cognitions, alcohol consumption, and negative consequences. The positive associations between sharing alcohol-related content and drinking (Litt et al., 2018) among young people on social networking sites, such as organizing going out, posting photos of themselves drinking, partying, having fun, are integral to the creation of both intoxigenic social identities and intoxigenic digital spaces. This new spatial frontier allows young people to (co-)construct their identities by sharing their nights out, by having photos and stories told and retold, and by being used in subtle and sophisticated ways by alcohol marketers. Through online quizzes and associations with alcohol brands, the expansion of drinking spaces reinforces normative intoxication while creating group affiliation. Intoxigenic digital spaces serve to expand young people's places of drinking by normalizing heavy drinking and increasing exposure to commercial interests (Lindsay & Supski, 2017: 52).

The way users can interact with alcohol ads on social media should be further regulated. This means that the interactive features of Facebook and other social media communities, apart from the simpler content posted online, have implications for the cultural acceptance of alcohol and drinking behavior. This should be considered in legislation and codes of practice dealing with commercial communications about alcohol (WHO, 2020: 5). Digital behaviors (e.g., postings about alcohol) related to an individual's self-reported drinking cognitions, alcohol consumption, and negative consequences can also be used for public health surveillance and interventions (Litt et al., 2018).

References

Alcohol Factsheet. (2015). Geneva: World Health Organization. Retrieved August 24, 2021 from http://www.who.int/mediacentre/factsheets/fs349/en

Boers, E., Afzali, M. H. & Conrod, P. (2020). A longitudinal study on the relationship between screen time and adolescent alcohol use: The mediating role of social norms. *Preventive Medicine, 132*(105992), 1–6. Retrieved August 24, 2021 from https://pubmed.ncbi.nlm.nih.gov/31954144/

Briefing: Protecting Children and Young People from Alcohol Marketing. (2019). Alcohol Focus Scotland. Retrieved August 24, 2021, from https://www.alcohol-focus-scotland.org.uk/media/310885/public-protecting-children-and-young-people-from-alcohol-marketing-sep19.pdf

Lindsay, J., & Supski, S. (2017). Curating identity. Drinking, young women, femininities and social media practices. In A. C. Lyons, T. McCreanor, I. Goodwin, & H. M. Barnes (Eds.), *Youth drinking cultures in a digital world: Alcohol, social media and cultures of intoxication.* Routledge.

Litt, D. M., Lewis, M. A., Spiro, E. S., Aulck, L., Waldron, K. A., Head-Corliss, M. K., & Swanson, A. (2018). #drunktwitter: Examining the relations between alcohol-related twitter content and alcohol willingness and use among underage young adults. *Drug and Alcohol Dependence, 193*, 75–82.

WHO. (2020). *Alcohol marketing in the WHO European Region. Update report on the evidence and recommended policy actions*. Retrieved August 24, 2021 from https://movendi.ngo/wp-content/uploads/2020/07/WH24_FOBBS_Marketing_online.pdf

Chapter 9
Masculinity and Practices of Drinking

It isn't chic for women to be drunk. Men drunks are more excusable, more easily absolved, but why? It must be thought they have better reasons.

Margaret Atwood, Cat's Eye.

Abstract The reasons for alcohol use differ by gender. The alcohol industry appeals to men differently than it does to women due to entrenched gender stereotypes. The reasons why men are more inclined to drink alcohol, intoxication practices, the embodiment of masculinity, the expression of identities, and the role of social media are all discussed in this chapter. With technological advancements, the alcohol industry encourages men to drink to satisfy their thirst for power, knowing that those men who are particularly preoccupied with personal power would drink more heavily. Drunkenness and drinking have long been related to masculine identities associated with characteristics like autonomy, independence, bodily composure, control, self-discipline, and strength. Social media has contributed in the mainstream of alcohol use and binge drinking by offering fertile, uncontrolled ground for the marketing and branding of alcohol goods.

The main reason men drink is to satisfy their need for a sense of power. Men drink primarily to feel more powerful. Those for whom personal power is a particular concern drink more heavily (Douglas, 2010: 8). Drinking and drunkenness are traditionally masculine practices associated with masculine identities and socially constructed ideals of masculinity such as autonomy, independence, bodily composure, control, self-discipline, and strength. Excessive drinking, especially beer drinking and drinking in public are ways in which men demonstrate hegemonic masculinity. Hegemonic masculinity is a dominant position constructed in relation to femininities and subordinated masculinities. It is about the maintenance of power within and between social configurations of gender. It is dynamic, and although most men do not embody it, it is a contextual form of masculinity that many men aspire to. In this way, it is distinct from other local masculinities, particularly subordinated

M. Ramšak, *Social Impact of Wine Marketing*, Contributions to Management Science, https://doi.org/10.1007/978-3-030-89224-1_9

masculinities, and functions to legitimize patriarchal social relations. For example, drinking lots of beer as opposed to gin is a conventional way of distinguishing real men from women or gay men (Lyons & Gough, 2016: 66).

A key feature of drinking to demonstrate hegemonic masculinity is the ability to tolerate alcohol. Hegemonic masculinity is associated with the control of embodied drunkenness that occurs after excessive drinking. Thus, it is important for men to "hold" one's drink and effects such as slurring, stumbling, and passing out are seen as signs of weakness (Lyons and Gough 2016: 66–67). Men are judged by how well they carry their drink and how generously they spend on drink (Douglas, 2010: 8). However, many young people, both men and women, socialize and drink together with the explicit aim of getting drunk and losing bodily control and memory. Drinking and drunkenness are attractive to (young) men because they provide an enjoyable release from the constant, everyday imperative to control the male body. Idealized male bodies are controlled, rational, autonomous, and independent, and drinking and drunkenness can provide men with a coveted escape from such embodied performances. Young men may need to negotiate the dichotomy of control/release; while drinking as a release can be seen as masculine, there is an increasing (neoliberal) requirement for individuals to be health conscious and responsible. In practice, this may mean being sensible (controlled, e.g., going to the gym) during the week and letting loose and getting drunk at the weekend (Lyons and Gough 2016: 67–68).

The more alcohol is used as a sign of selection and exclusion, the more its abuse can be expected to appear in the ranks of the excluded. A man suffering from social rejection would understandably turn to compensatory drinking in order to possess at least the symbol of what he does not have. A man's rise from outsider to established insider depends as much on his role as drinking buddy as on his skills and work effort (Douglas, 2010: 9; Heath, 2010: 31, 38, 45). Alcohol addiction adds to the despair of the person who already sees himself as an outsider and is about to be excluded. Transcultural contact also influenced drinking, with a sharp increase in alcohol consumption often accompanied by pressure to acculturate. Exclusion takes many forms, some of them very subtle. Wine connoisseurship, for example, is in itself a field for competition. Connoisseurship also has its own power for social dominance (Douglas, 2010: 9, 10).

Drinking alcohol allows men to engage with aspects of embodiment traditionally denied in idealized masculinity, such as experiencing and expressing emotions, pain, and friendship. Drinking in the pub is an act of friendship that allows men to explicitly display and discuss emotions and mental health. Alcohol enables young men and women to cross gender boundaries, with young men talking about how alcohol created a context that allowed them to engage in behaviors that were seen as non-masculine (e.g., crying and being emotional) or homosexual. Alcohol consumption can therefore allow men to transcend notions of every day, idealized (heterosexual) masculinity and its embodiment, and engage in gender performances that go against proscribed gender practices (Lyons and Gough 2016: 68).

The relationship between traditional masculine identities and alcohol (particularly beer) appears to be alive and strong in some contexts, while in others resistant or alternative ways of constructing gender identities in relation to alcohol consumption are evident. Given changes in drinking cultures, including the rise of women's public drinking, the diversity of drinking venues and products, and the increasing accessibility and availability of alcohol, it is perhaps not surprising that masculinity is being redefined in relation to alcohol consumption. Additionally, more diverse forms of alcohol consumption may still define traditional masculinities. For example, the increase in craft beer consumption may be related to changing masculine identities among (older) middle-class men, who may thus distinguish themselves from (younger) working class lager drinkers. There may also be alternative ways in which men construct their gender identities, particularly in relation to femininity and the rise in female consumption. Men are also drinking more different alcoholic products than in the past (not just beer) (Lyons and Gough 2016: 66–67).

There is also a difference in spending habits between men and women. Single men spend a greater proportion of their spending on food consumed away from home, alcohol, transportation, entertainment, tobacco, and on retirement investments than single women. Single women spend a larger share of their spending on food consumed at home, housing, clothing, healthcare, personal care, and reading materials. Both groups of singles use the Internet more than other consumers. There is a desire to reduce shopping time and use the time for other activities (Michman & Mazze, 2006: 95).

The rapid rise of social media, particularly social networking sites, has led to drinking practices and cultures shifting to online spaces. Popular social networking platforms include Facebook, Twitter, Instagram, and YouTube. People use them to connect with others, explicitly articulate their social networks and make them visible. Young people use social networks extensively, sharing their drinking events, experiences, and practices through posts, status updates, check-ins, likes, photos, and videos. Sharing drinking events, experiences, and alcohol-related content on Facebook serves to consolidate friendship bonds, create drinking cultures that are airbrushed, minimize the visibility of negative consequences and also enables (gendered) identity work. It additionally intensifies the normalization of alcohol and drinking to intoxication and provides a fertile (unregulated) context for the marketing and branding of alcohol products (e.g., brand pages on social media, events, and competitions that encourage user interaction with the brand (Lyons and Gough 2016: 68).

Young people use social networking sites to share their tastes and preferences, stay connected with friends and broader peer groups, display social connections, and perform social identities. Social media use is a gendered activity, and it has always been employed by users to construct and perform gendered identities. Technology has historically been identified with masculinity and masculine competencies. Gendered assumptions about technology may mean that, for example, women distance themselves from technology as a way to construct feminine identities while men appropriate technology to "do masculinity." However, such simplistic alignments of masculinities with technology may become more complicated with the rise of social networking technologies. Online gender performances on social networking sites reflect traditional notions of masculinity and femininity and self-presentation mirror stereotypical gender norms, for example, that women portray themselves as attractive and affiliative, and men as embody strength and power (Lyons and Gough 2016: 69).

References

Douglas, M. (2010). A distinctive anthropological perspective. In *Constructive drinking. Perspectives on drink from anthropology. Mary Douglas collected works, volume X* (pp. 3–15). Routledge.

Heath, D. (2010). A decade of development in the anthropological study of alcohol use, 1970–1980. In *Constructive drinking. Perspectives on drink from anthropology. Mary Douglas collected works, volume X* (pp. 16–69). Routledge.

Lyons AC, Gough B (2016) Masculinities, alcohol consumption and social networking. In: Lyons A, McCreanor T, Goodwin I, Barnes HM (eds) *Youth drinking cultures in a digital world. Alcohol, social media and cultures of intoxication*. Routledge, pp 66–79

Michman, R. D., & Mazze, E. M. (2006). *The affluent consumer: Marketing and selling the luxury lifestyle*. Praeger Publishers.

Chapter 10
Drinking Games

Later he'll be drunk in extremis and will only be able to speak the Esperanto of alcoholics, which is a language full of stuttering from the geological layers of our animal ancestors.

Anaïs Nin, A Spy in the House of Love

Abstract Drinking games have been around for a long time, but they were not the competitive drinking games that gave rise to the contemporary bingeing, hazing, peer pressure, and competitive drinking culture. The chapter discusses drinking games as a type of social drinking that relies on the drinker's resilience. It begins with an overview of the past, including various analog varieties, and then goes on to discuss contemporary digital counterparts such as multimedia games, binge applications, online quizzes, YouTube series on binge games, and other forms found in the alcohol industry and spreading as social epidemics.

The alcohol industry offers a variety of multilingual multimedia games, online quizzes, and mobile apps. A drinking game, for example, is a high-risk, social drinking activity that has certain rules (i.e., when to drink and how much to consume). It is designed to promote intoxication and requires participants to perform cognitive and/or motor task. Drinking games are unlike other high-risk drinking activities (e.g., prepartying, or drinking before going out) because by following the rules, certain players may be targeted to drink more than others, leading to their more rapid intoxication. Drinking games are prevalent among college students who are aware of the health risks associated with heavy drinking, but this knowledge does not deter them from playing drinking games (Zamboanga et al., 2015).

Drinking games or bingeing games which involve the consumption of alcoholic beverages emerge in many ways. They can be pub games, played in bars, inns, and taverns, particularly in England, tabletop games, including card games, and today,

M. Ramšak, *Social Impact of Wine Marketing*, Contributions to Management Science, https://doi.org/10.1007/978-3-030-89224-1_10

especially popular apps with drinking games.[1] Drinking games have been banned in some educational institutions because of the health and moral consequences, including the tendency to depict violence, sexism, sexual violence, and encouragement of alcoholism.

Drinking games have been around for a long time. *Kottabos* was a popular ancient Greek game in which the goal was to fling the lees or residue from the bottom of your terracotta wine glass and hit a disk balanced on a small pole. Another popular drinking "game" was competitive improvised speechmaking on a specific theme. This is demonstrated in Plato's Symposium, where each participant is required to deliver a speech in praise of love while drinking wine. The judge was said to be Dionysus, the god of wine. However, there is a significant difference between today's games. Those are "competitive" drinking games, but they are not the "competitive drinking" games that are popular in and around universities today, where the winner, loser, or both can get extremely drunk. Evidence suggests that these emerged in southern Germany during the Reformation, in the early 1530s, when the medieval way of life began to falter but young men were still training to become knights. The Crusades were long over, and as military tactics evolved, so did the economy. There was no obvious outlet for their energies because there were no obvious job prospects or a specific purpose to their lives. They appear to have turned to wine to fill the void. And, with Germany's vineyards four times larger than they are today—and per capita consumption six times higher—the temptation to overindulge was strong (Fontaine, 2020). Drinking games and toxic masculinity may seem like regrettable modern phenomena but the two have gone hand-in-hand for centuries. Competitive drinking and rowdy behavior among privileged young men are rooted in the debauches of testosterone-fueled youths deprived of knightly pursuits. Copious consumption, bragging of sexual prowess, and tavern brawls were all par for the course on a night out (Bridge, 2020). The author, Vincent Obsopoeus (ca. 1498–1539), the rector of an elite school in Ansbach, wrote the first two books of his three-part poem, *The Art of Drinking* (*De Arte Bibendi*) (1536), ostensibly in an effort to halt this poisonous new culture. In the wine-lands of sixteenth-century Germany, he witnessed the birth of a poisonous new culture of bingeing, hazing, peer pressure, and competitive drinking. In part three, however, the mask slips and Obsopoeus instead tells us how to win drinking games, citing extensive personal experience—and the games he describes in it are the first to look recognizably familiar. Games in which, for example, the objective was to take drinks in alternation until the other person passes out. The last one standing is the winner. The remainder of book three details strategies to win. When in a competition, Obsopoeus says to use full bottles to put the pressure on. The secret to winning these games is simple. There is no magic that will increase your tolerance or stretch your stomach. Rather, the

[1]For example, iPuke, Heads Up!, Drink and Tell, Seven, Game of Shots, Drinking Game by EvilBit, Picolo drinking game, Never Have I Ever, Truth or Shots, Truth or Dare, Truth or Drink, Kings, Drink-O-Tron, Drink or Doom, Circle of Death, King of Booze, The King's Cup, Bomba Drink, Drinking Wheel.

trick to the art of drinking, is making sure your opponent matches your drink-for-drink each and every time (Fontaine, 2020). The poem, banned by the Catholic Church, recommends taking tactical toilet breaks and tipping waiters to water down wine. Germany already had fraternities back then and they clearly liked to party. When they got drunk, they violated all the same taboos that people violate today. Later, a 1612 book *The Law of Drinking*, told how Oxford students take their liquor out of chamber pots (Pattinson, 2020).

One of the analogous forms of the drinking game is the toast, for wine is part of the daily and festive diet, it is present in the customs of work and the year, it toasts nature and her bounties, the beginning and the end of a cycle of work.

Toast is a word from the English language, a lightly toasted slice of bread. In earlier times, the people of the British Isles would dip a slice of bread toasted over a fire in alcohol to give it a grainy aroma and flavor. Later, the tradition of dipping toast fell into disuse, but another was born: "toasting" before drinking. A toast is now a ritual, one of the genres of table etiquette, along with a small talk, a song and, in some cases, greetings and farewells (Rychkov, 2015: 187). Its main functions are: to communicate or exchange certain information between people at the table; to integrate, because a special unity is felt by people in the process of making a toast when they touch glasses and drink together; to differentiate, because the consumption of the food and drink becomes a means of social identification, such as, e.g., status, age, gender, toast giver/recipient; and to maintain continuity because a toast offers the transmission of cultural values from generation to generation through symbolic behavior. This characteristic is most evident in the adherence to etiquette accepted by this group of people (Rychkov, 2015: 188). In addition to the direct invitation to drink, numerous toasts congratulate, express the wish for health, longevity, praise the vines and wine, flirt, make us laugh, etc. The toasts are known all over the world, their texts adapt to the situation. For personal anniversaries, the most popular toasts are those that directly address and toast the celebrant, and those with repetitive forms that attract the attention of everyone present and encourage them to drink the wine to the bottom, so that the table is well intoxicated by the end of the toast. A toast to the celebrant with solemn words and alcohol is an integral part of the celebration.

Drinking games apps promise relaxation and self-indulgence, of course, only if the player drinks a certain amount of alcohol. The games require players to have a mobile app that establishes relationships between them, dictates the speed of reactions, sets a penalty with the number of glasses or sips of alcohol drunk. These games are based on drinking endurance, reaction speed to the rules of the game, certain skills, observation, etc. Mobile drinking games are graphically and aurally appealing, include mobile playing cards, recognizable characters, allusions to historical events, are sometimes sexually, historically, and geographically oriented, are adapted to different levels of difficulty, and include an unlimited number of players. The greater the drunkenness of the players, the more difficult it is to win in binge apps and the more binge penalties they receive. Moreover, the mobile apps impose additional self-deprecating penalties on drinkers in cases of revealing their weaknesses and past recklessness, mostly in the sexual sphere.

The Internet also offers ideas for numerous analog drinking games that require few props besides alcohol, such as chairs, a deck of cards, music, and friends. These drinking games involve a "punishment" for losers, i.e., drinking a certain amount of alcohol (from one to several units or glasses of alcohol). Some games are designed to have players "seek the truth" (e.g., Truth or Shots and Truth or Dare) and are based on the hit YouTube series Truth or Drink, which has over 500 million views. The rules are simple: you provide the drinks and shuffle together the decks of cards of your choice. Then you draw a card and ask the questions printed on it. Depending on the answer, you get a nice stiff drink or tell the cold, hard truth. By the end of the night, the players are better friends after asking the questions they never would have dared to ask out loud. The questions on the cards escalate from relaxing to extra dirty to questions that put the players' relationship to the ultimate test. In the game, you find out things you never wanted to know about your colleagues, family, friends, and significant other. Such drinking card games are meant to test the boundaries with friends, family, or those the player loves. The only thing standing between the player and the ultimate truth is a bottle.

The games are also printed as booklets and available on the Internet. The colophon of the booklets contains warnings that excessive alcohol consumption can be harmful to health, that the publisher urges caution and restraint in engaging in practices related to the activities depicted in the book, and that the book is intended for adults only. The publisher also washes its hands of the matter and points out that it cannot accept responsibility for the result of the use or misuse of the book or for any loss, injury, or damage caused thereby. This is an example of compliance with alcohol consumption regulations and at the same time an open disregard in favor of the alcohol industry.

One example of an epidemic of crazy drinking games is "icing," which swept among American students and other 20-year-old men in the first decade of the twenty-first century and began to decline in 2010, when Smirnoff was supposed to wipe out the infamous and sadistic website "BrosIcingBros" because the drinking game is not supposed to be in line with their marketing code (Goodman, 2010; Quittner, 2010; Lindstrom, 2011: 107). The premise of the world's biggest viral drinking game is simple: "First, you give a friend a can of Smirnoff Ice malt beverage. Said friend then has to balance the can on his knee and drink the whole thing at once. The only way to avoid becoming a victim of this uncertain fate is to carry a bottle yourself, in which case you have to drink both bottles – before, of course, going out and 'icing' someone else. Sounds absolutely awful, yet somehow this game quickly infected college campuses around the country, spawned several Web sites, and, according to the *New York Times*, 'explode[d] from obscurity into a bizarre pastime for college kids, Wall Streeters and minor celebrities.' Smirnoff has emphatically denied that it bears any responsibility for 'icing', but regardless, it's been quite lucrative for the company. As the *Times* reports, the phenomenon has not only raised awareness of the brand but also extended it to young men who formerly saw Ice as 'girly' and feminine. And sales of Ice products almost immediately took off in some Southern college towns, where the game took early root. The point is, whether it emerges organically or is deliberately orchestrated by marketers, peer pressure delivers a windfall for brands and companies" (Lindstrom, 2011: 107). Such hijacking of a brand is not uncommon, and in this case, it has produced a short-term benefit for Smirnoff, raising awareness of the brand and extending it to young male consumers who formerly shunned the drink as one aimed at women (Goodman, 2010). Sales have grown especially in the southern states of the United States, where the game also originates. Either way, whether the game develops on its own, or is prompted by one or another marketing ploy, peer pressure is a gold mine for brands and companies.

This is exactly why companies of all stripes have become so skilled at planting the seeds of social epidemics and then sitting back to watch them grow (as Smirnoff was accused of doing in this case). The most persuasive marketing messages are not magazine ads or TV commercials or billboards; they are the ones that come from—or at least seem to come from—our peers. In fact, one of the most effective—and sneakiest—viral marketing strategies is for a company to create a blog or YouTube video that is so extreme, funny, outrageous, provocative, or frightening (or a combination of the above) that it raises the question, is this a joke, or is it real? (Lindstrom, 2011: 107). The game has exposed the mercurial line between guerrilla advertising and genuine social media trends, raising questions about how young consumers can know when they have co-opted a brand for their own purposes, and when that brand has co-opted them (Goodman, 2010).

References

Bridge, M. (2020, 20 July). Now that's a rowdy knight on the tiles: A poem has revealed the centuries-old roots of drinking games, bragging and brawls. *The Times*. Retrieved August 24, 2021 from https://www.thetimes.co.uk/article/now-thats-a-rowdy-knight-on-the-tiles-2dsn36227

Fontaine, M. (2020, 3 July). The rules of drinking: The long history of drinking games – and how to win them. *History Today*. Retrieved August 24, 2021 from https://www.historytoday.com/history-matters/rules-drinking

Goodman, D. J. (2010). Popular new drinking game raises question, who's 'Icing' whom? *New York Times* June 9. Retrieved August 24, 2021 from https://www.nytimes.com/2010/06/09/business/media/09adco.html

Lindstrom, M. (2011). *Brandwashed: Tricks companies use to manipulate our minds and persuade us to buy*. Crown Business.

Pattinson, R. (2020, 21 July). You're Bad! British blokes have been binge-drinking 'since the 15th century'. *The Sun*. Retrieved August 24, 2021 from https://www.thesun.co.uk/news/12178853/men-binge-boozing-games-since-15th-century-tudor/

Quittner, E. (2010, 17 June). Bro culture: Icing on the social-marketing cake? *Time*. Retrieved August 24, 2021 from http://content.time.com/time/nation/article/0,8599,1997489,00.html

Rychkov, S. (2015). Magic of a toast. In T. Minniyakhmetova & K. Velkoborská (Eds.), *Magic in rituals and rituals in magic. The yearbook of the SIEF (Société Internationale d'Ethnologie et de folklore) working group on the ritual year; the ritual year 10* (pp. 187–193). ELM Scholarly Press.

Zamboanga, B. L., Agaloos Pesigan, I. J., Tomaso, C. C., Schwartz, S. J., Ham, L. S., Bersamin, M., Kim, S. Y., Cano, M. A., Castillo, L. G., Forthun, L. F., Krauss Whitbourne, S. & Hurley, E. A.

(2015). Frequency of drinking games participation and alcohol-related problems in a multiethnic sample of college students: Do gender and ethnicity matter? *Addictive Behaviors*, *41*, 112–116. Retrieved August 24, 2021 from https://www.semanticscholar.org/paper/Frequency-of-drinking-games-participation-and-in-a-Zamboanga-Pesigan/601fe267c675b6ab872792446d4cc6eec14ca069

Chapter 11
Digital Marketing Strategies during a Coronavirus Pandemic

I want a new liver to replace my heart.
Um, why?
Because then I could drink more and care less.

L.A. Casey, Alec

Abstract During the coronavirus crisis, alcohol was a balm for isolation and a tool for human connection. This chapter presents how the coronavirus pandemic in 2020 and 2021 created unprecedented circumstances for the alcohol business, as the world was forced to close its doors to prevent the disease from spreading. The pandemic accelerated the adoption of digital technology in the alcohol sector. Online remote alcohol sales, online wine tastings, blind tastings, mobile app delivery options, a larger production and better e-marketing of canned wines, YouTube promotions, and Zoom drinking games have all arisen as new or improved marketing strategies. The examples provided demonstrate how resourceful and flexible the alcohol industry is, allowing it to flourish despite adversities.

During and after the pandemic, when many of the social structures and activities that people relied on to maintain their well-being were compromised, we saw an increase in many mental health problems, and the use of alcohol was one of the coping mechanisms for desperate times. Stressed, anxious, and isolated people increased their alcohol consumption to numb the uncertain future, which made them even more anxious as alcohol is a depressant, both physically and mentally.

Since then, alcohol has been a silent, constant presence underlying the larger story of the pandemic, in ways that alternately celebrate and condemn its role in our lives. Throughout the coronavirus crisis when alcohol was both a balm for isolation and a tool for human connection, it also posed a greater than normal danger to some people in recovery. The pandemic situation was a precursor to another binge (Mobley, 2021). People were pushed to create home drinking occasions fast and ingeniously as a result of the outbreak. COVID-19's impact on consumption habits was likely only equaled in the early twentieth century by Prohibition. Virtual

M. Ramšak, *Social Impact of Wine Marketing*, Contributions to Management Science, https://doi.org/10.1007/978-3-030-89224-1_11

stand-ins and at-home occasions have taken the place of after-work cocktails, dinners, and weekend brunches. People have developed a taste for drinking while cooking and for live-streaming entertainment (Morris, 2021).

Although the world had to shut down and the economic impact of the lockdown put liquor stores in a financially threatening position as the hospitality industry had to close the doors of liquor stores and restaurants, the alcohol industry was not sleeping. The pandemic was the accelerator of digitization in all industries; in the alcohol industry, it accelerated new marketing techniques that relied on online remote alcohol sales.

Lockdown gave way to the development of e-commerce sites and delivery strategies that allowed them to stay afloat. The liquor industry not only managed to stay afloat, but increased their overall alcohol sales. This would not have been possible if liquor companies had not turned to e-commerce and added affordable and timely alcohol delivery options. Companies that also offered mobile apps for even more customer convenience had the most success. By allowing customers to search and order beer, wine, and spirits in a quick mobile app, these companies were able to grow their loyal customer base. With delivery options and a mobile app, liquor stores, bars, or distribution centers will continue to thrive, and artificial intelligence will play a big role in digital marketing efforts deployed through websites and apps. For every drink that could no longer be served, one was delivered instead (Gibson, 2021).

The numbers of online remote alcohol sales were dramatic. For instance, in the week of March 15, 2020, alcohol sales in the United States increased 55%; in the week of March 21, 2020, when many people were following protective orders, online alcohol sales increased 262%. In the area of San Francisco Bay, which had one of the earliest orders to stay home, residents reportedly drank 42% more than usual in the first week of the rule, and similarly, a home-breathalyzer company in the San Francisco Bay Area stated that it observed a 42% increase in blood alcohol levels among locals in the first week (NBC, 2020; Mobley, 2021; Chesler, 2020). Liquor stores, meanwhile, which were allowed to continue operating in most US states despite restrictions on many other businesses, saw an increase in sales (Chesler, 2020). In April 2020, 3000 Americans were surveyed nationwide for the Alcohol.org study, and 35% of them said they were likely to drink more alcohol while self-isolating; one-fifth (22%) of Americans said they hoarded alcohol for self-isolation before other foods and drinks. Many drinkers had that one drink they reached for during stressful times, and beer was the drink most commonly consumed by Americans in self-isolation, with 38% reporting this. This was followed by cocktails (26%), wine (21%), and spirits (15%). Broken down by gender, the most popular drink for men during self-isolation was found to be beer (44%), which is perhaps unsurprising. This was followed by wine (22%), spirits (22%), and cocktails (11%). In comparison, women were most likely to consume cocktails (38%) during isolation, followed by beer (33%), wine (24%), and spirits (5%). Residents of Hawaii were most likely to drink at home during working hours (67%), while Arkansas were least likely (8%) (Alcohol.org, 2020).

The marketing and sale of wine were forced to go online in order to survive during the coronavirus pandemic. Although there have been some successful online wine retailers who were more than a decade old, the wine trade has notoriously lagged behind in the use of online marketing communication tools (Lorch, 2020).

One difficulty is that sharing wine is social. Wine lovers prefer to be with their friends when they drink wine, or with their colleagues when they taste it. Wine producers and their importers value time together and may meet once or twice a year to share the latest vintages. With the COVID-19 crisis, not only was everyone literally isolated, but consumers could not visit winery tasting rooms or discover new wines through in-store or restaurant tastings for several weeks or even months; and both consumers and retailers lost the chance to taste and meet wine producers at countless cancelled or postponed wine shows because they were offered few alternative opportunities (Lorch, 2020).

The pandemic accelerated the digitalization of the wine industry—especially in the areas of communication and distribution. One result of this dynamic was the rapid spread of the modern way of tasting wine, online or virtual wine tasting, which was virtually unheard of before the pandemic and offered a completely new experience for consumers (Nilsson et al., 2021). Several independent online initiatives addressing this gap have emerged, some of them adaptations of existing online events, others created by experienced digital wine marketers (Lorch, 2020).

The pioneers of online wine tastings set a new standard and introduced an innovative tool that combined several objectives: contact with existing customers, attracting new customers, and entertaining and increasing sales. To gather reliable data, a global online survey was conducted in January 2021 with 1423 wineries from more than 40 countries. The goal of the survey was to assess the impact of the global pandemic on online wine tastings and to find out how wineries have changed their approach to wine tourism since the pandemic began and whether the concept of online wine tastings will continue and grow after a COVID-19 period. The survey asked about topics such as reasons for offering online wine tastings, profitability, structure of the new online tool, and many others. The results of the survey clearly show COVID-19's impact on the growing trend of online wine tasting usage and that this tool is more than just entertainment for wine lovers, but also has a tangible business aspect. The global interest in this innovative solution was reflected in the high number of participants (Nilsson et al., 2021).

The results of the study show that the size of the winery matters—the larger it is; the more online wine tastings were organized. However, the larger wineries also had the highest decrease in wine tasting visitors. The main reasons for offering online wine tastings were diverse and differed mainly according to the size of the winery. Zoom, as an online wine tasting platform, was the most popular. This can be explained by the fact that Zoom is a user-friendly platform that includes many useful features that presenters can use during the tasting. Moreover, no registration or download is necessary to start Zoom as a participant (Nilsson et al., 2021).

The research also showed some differences between the main target groups and the number of online wine tastings. For example, Germany had by far the highest number of business-to-consumer online wine tastings, where companies promoted their products and services to individuals. Other countries saw a higher proportion of business-to-business tastings, services, or information between businesses rather than between businesses and consumers. Wineries were also cautious about the number of online wine tastings. One in two wineries offered fewer than 6 online wine tastings and a third offered between 6 and 20. The majority of wineries that engaged in online wine tastings in 2020, plan to offer them in the future. Given that many wineries have been able to achieve their goals with online wine tastings—and 50% were even making a profit from them—it is not surprising that most of them plan to continue offering them in the future. Online wine tastings proved to be an excellent way to counter declining sales. More than half of the wineries that hosted online wine tastings rated them as profitable or very profitable. Higher profitability went hand-in-hand with a higher number of tastings conducted and participants, but also with the length of the tasting. Profitable wineries used more sales and marketing channels, tended to host tastings for larger groups, focused on business-to-consumer marketing, and hosted longer tastings (over 60 minutes instead of under 60 minutes) (Nilsson et al., 2021).

A Portuguese company that operates in the digital wine market, advising wineries on their online presence and running wine fairs and events that often include a digital element, had planned a campaign in the United States to help Portuguese producers meet importers. Plans were postponed when the wine tariff crisis erupted. The company was already working on ideas to facilitate online meetings when the Prowein, the world's leading trade fair for wines and spirits in Germany was canceled. The company decided to help growers who had planned meetings thereby launching the online event Portugal Wine Week, which took place in March 2020, when Prowein was scheduled to take place. Portugal Wine Week had two activities: a two-day live stream program and one-on-one twenty-minute online video meetings between winemakers and importers throughout the week. Originally, winemakers were to stay in hotel rooms in Lisbon and Porto, but since self-isolation became necessary, winemakers participated remotely from their homes or wineries. They were taught how to use the Zoom video application for a live chat and tasting. None of the 62 Portuguese winemakers had done a live online tasting before. Virtual meetings with importers, in addition to learning new skills, were a great opportunity for the producers and they thanked the company that organized them. Some continued to hold live tastings with their customers and it is a massive behavioral change by winemakers, although some wine marketers warned that this should not be seen as a replacement for wine fairs in the future, but as complementary events (Lorch, 2020).

Similarly, a new niche for the general public, especially the young, evolved in an attempt to alleviate everyone's isolation a little during the lockdowns, but ultimately to sell the alcohol that was not drunk, which we can call unsophisticated wine drinking. Blind tastings (guessing) of wines based on color, scents, and flavors to determine the grape, age, and provenance, reviews of lousy wine, junk food wine or champagne pairings, idiot guides to wine, and promoting such activity on YouTube were among the activities. For example, the idea that wine is snobby and elitist has been turned on its head by the trend of pairing junk food with wine or champagne even before pandemic. Junk food is consumed with alcohol at sporting events, game nights, or other social gatherings, but the 2020 pandemic has created a very specific niche for home drinking that pairs wines that are not common, just off the radar, with food, like sweet or savory snacks, cotton candy, chocolate brownies, churros, waffles, donuts, white chocolate covered pretzels, cinnamon and chocolate chip cookies, popcorn, corn dogs, peanut butter cups, grilled banana, and Nutella sandwich with brie, breakfast cereal, ice cream in wine, French fries, potato chips, bacon-wrapped foods, chicken nuggets, jalapeño poppers, deep-fried mozzarella sticks, donut burgers, and cheese crackers. Some winemakers tried to preserve the social elements of wine in the digital world by promising to entertain a young(er) audience and make wine interesting by offering nonsense—culturally and in terms of the wines they brought to market.

What began in 2003 with The Family Coppola's—a 187-milliliter can—and took years to gain a foothold in the market and grow rapidly year after year, got a much-needed boost during the coronavirus pandemic.

For years, canned wine was a non-category; over time, it slowly evolved into a fad until it qualified as a full-fledged wine category that continues to grow. Canned wine sales are on the rise as suppliers, distributors, retailers, and most importantly, consumers (especially younger consumers 21 and older) are becoming more accustomed to and receptive of canned wines (Williams, 2019). Canned wines are becoming more popular by the day, and the data suggests that this will be a long-lasting trend, not a fad. Due to the success of the growing canned wine category, many producers have decided to launch their own labels. Wine companies expanded the category to include premium wines, e.g., 2015 wines from organically farmed vineyards, vineyard-specific, varietal-specific, vintage-specific wines, canned rosés, carbonated canned products, e.g., blends such as spritzers, rosé sparkling wines, Riesling radlers and other wine-based cocktails. Wineries saw endless opportunities in on-the-go wine cans as consumers range from wine novices to beer lovers looking for a portable way to take wine outdoors or on the go, as well as for those who want to drink a glass without committing to a bottle; 375 milliliters equals about 2.5 glasses of wine (Williams, 2019). Consumer desire for 187 ml and 250 ml in single-serve cans is strong, but wine in cans is limited to 187 ml, 250 ml, 375 ml, or 500 ml cans in the United States by the Alcohol and Tobacco Tax and Trade Bureau, which regulates the sale and trade of wine, with 187 ml and 250 ml sold only as multiples (Williams et al., 2018: 8).

Canned wine is also making its way into restaurants and is marketed in places where wine is not traditionally served (stadiums, beach and swimming pools, boating clubs, zoos, botanical gardens, etc.) and is also sold in vending machines (Williams et al., 2018: 19). Five main (themes) stimulate interest and drive the expansion of the wine-in-can market: convenience, occasion expansion, sustainability/cost savings, quality, and visual image/branding. Each theme is complex, multidimensional, and in some cases overlaps with one or more of the other drivers. Perhaps the most important driver of the canned wine market is convenience, but it is strongly linked to occasion expansion (Williams et al., 2018: 21). The Internet is full of selfies of customers next to colorful, creative canned wine, less so than selfies next

Fig. 11.1 A Facebook self-promotion for a spritzer in a can, one of the wine products by a Slovene wine-growing and winemaking family that they brought on summer vacation. Source: With permission from Vinoreja Kaučič, Slovenia, August 2021

to bottles of wine. The fun, progressive, festive nature of many designer cans inspires social media blog posts, hashtags, selfies, and pictures of friends enjoying these single- or double-serve cans (Williams et al., 2018: 26).

Canned wine continues to be one of the fastest-growing wine categories in the United States. Volume sales reached $253 million in the 52 weeks ending March 20, 2021, up 62% from the previous 12 months (Romano, 2021). There was also a trend towards canned ready-to-drink beverages after the 2020 lockdown. (e.g., Fig. 11.1 shows a Facebook self-promotion for a spritzer in a can, one of the wine products taken on vacation by a Slovene wine-growing and winemaking family in August 2021.) There was strong interest from caterers to get back on track, and cans were a convenient product because people kept it simple with COVID-19 measures in bars. The international market demanded cans as an easy serving medium (Mileham, 2021).

For example, one million Portonic cans were produced in the first year after the pandemic began because demand was high (Mileham, 2021). The newly created Portonic subcategory had a strong, positive response from several markets. By May 2021, Portonic cans were available in the main supermarket chains in Portugal and initial sales were extremely encouraging, while international markets such as the United Kingdom and the United States showed strong interest. In the United Kingdom market, interest has been highest in the independent sector and mid-sized supermarkets, as large supermarkets often take longer to analyze the potential. Consumers found it convenient and Portonic opened up consumption moments that might not have existed for Port before. It was much easier to throw a six- or twelve-pack in the cooler to take to the beach or fishing than to pack the bottle of Port, tonics, mixers, and glasses (Mileham, 2021).

When the coronavirus swept around the world in 2020, bars, pubs, and clubs were closed, the physical distance was demanded, many virtual drinking games appeared. The pandemic began with so much fear that it was only a matter of time before drinking games found a new function in quarantine. Drinking games, by their basic nature, were not meant to function remotely. But in the pandemic, apps like FaceTime, Hangouts, Houseparty, and Zoom provided the framework for a virtual social life, and players adapted to the new environment. Virtual drinking games and game rules became popular fairly early in the pandemic, only about a month after the pandemic was declared in March 2020, and the alcohol industry found a way to promote binge drinking with "friends" or colleagues anywhere in the shutdown world by inventing a virtual happy hour.

In the quarantine era, when social contact was not allowed and people craved human closeness, the time was ripe for Zoom drinking games like Never Have I Ever, Quiplash, Cup Pong, Would You Rather, Most Likely To, Truth or Shots, Power Hour, Wizard Staff, Zoom Flip Cup, Drunk Pirate, Boozy Zoom Bingo, Scavenger Hunt, Blackout Truth Or Dare, Safari, Synonyms, Rhymes, Pet Peeves, This or That, Ride the Bus, Trivia, and others (Thompson, 2020; 14 Zoom Drinking Games, 2021). Five hundred years after Obsopoeus, in his cautionary words about Happy Hour, he advises that it is the wrong time and place for anger, sadness, or fear. Therefore, he said, Happy Hour Rule No.1 is to be a model of diplomacy in your behavior and speech. Even after so long, his tips are sound (Fontaine, 2020).

Zoom's virtual drinking games that involve the consumption of alcohol have their own rules. Players must take a sip when prompted by the rules or other players. Participants play these games during video calls. Most players use wine, beer, or spirits. However, they can also play with nonalcoholic beverages or use physical challenges instead (14 Zoom Drinking Games, 2021). Zoom drinking game rules apply in a virtual meeting or happy hour.

For example:

Take 1 drink.

For every mention of coronavirus.

Every time someone starts a meeting with "How are you?"

Every time someone says, "Sorry, I was on mute."

For every time zone represented.

Fig. 11.2 In 2020, news of the coronavirus was quickly picked up by "memers" on social media, who created a plethora of funny images linking Corona brand beer to the disease. The reaction from most viewers was that they have been drinking Corona for years, so they must be immune to it. The visual messages of Corona (beer) did not sink the company; on the contrary, its new fame only brought it more revenue. Source: A visual of unknown origin circulating on Facebook at the start of the 2020 epidemics

Every time someone talks over someone else.

Every person who is not wearing pants.

Take 2 drinks.

Every time someone attends a meeting and Spotify is still on.

Every time someone uses a fake background.

Every time someone comments on the fake background.

Take 3 drinks.

Every time someone changes locations in the middle of a meeting.

Every time someone has a laptop sitting on their body so they are constantly moving.

Take 4 drinks.

Any time a pet/child/significant other/roommate is disruptive in any way (Slaughter, 2021).

Since the epidemics began, social media has been flooded with jokes and memes of all kinds. Some of them referred to the Corona brand of beer (See Fig. 11.2). The Coronavirus situation did not hurt their brand, which was the subject of an absurd, never-ending stream of jokes and memes comparing it to the similarly named but completely unrelated virus. The company did nothing visible, but actively monitored what was going on behind the scenes, such as whether any misinformation and stronger correlations between the Corona brand and the disease emerged. The company did not assume that anyone truthfully believed that the beer was actually spreading the virus, and therefore did not need to take any action. That could change, depending on whether the jokes turn into a conspiracy theory and whether accounts with tens of thousands of followers on social media share them. But consumers understood there was no connection between the virus and the beer business. By mid-2021, that decision proved to be the right one, as predictably brand value dropped somewhat even in the midst of the coronavirus pandemic, as social distancing, forced venue closures, and lack of opportunity led to a total loss for the top 50 beer brands. Despite the unfortunate name association, Corona held on to the top spot despite the drop in brand value (Ferreira, 2020; Smith, 2021).

Funny sayings and "clever thoughts" with false claims on alcohol and coronavirus were also offered on glasses, mugs, and tumblers during the pandemic. They were personalized to encourage drinking in isolation, e.g., "Stuck Inside With My Wine," "Quarantine & Chill," "Alcohol Kills Germs," "Because COVID-19," "Whatever"; some inscriptions alluded only indirectly to the coronavirus "Sip Happens," "Let's Wine About It" (Mertes, 2021), but by and large their intent was to keep the drinks flowing. Such online drinking glass offerings were common because isolation or working from home was the perfect time for the alcohol industry to try to change people's behavior and drinking habits.

In memes on social media (Facebook and Twitter), the idea that alcohol destroys viruses was particularly prevalent. For example, in the first wave in March 2020, self-isolation was depicted as an image of a dead drunk lying in a wine cellar; a year later, when vaccines became available globally, the vaccine Russian Sputnik was compared to a man with a glass of vodka. These two images often circulated on Facebook and were commented on as saying that we should rely more on "folk remedies."

According to the World Health Organization, common myths about alcohol and COVID-19 are that drinking alcohol destroys the virus that causes COVID-19, that drinking strong alcohol kills the virus in the inhaled air, and that alcohol (beer, wine, distilled spirits, or herbal alcohol) stimulates immunity and resistance to the virus. The truth is that the consumption of alcohol does not destroy the virus, and that its consumption probably increases the health risks if a person becomes infected with the virus. Alcohol (at a concentration of at least 60% by volume) acts as a disinfectant on the skin, but it has no such effect on the body when ingested. Consumption of alcohol does not kill the virus in the inhaled air; it does not disinfect the mouth and throat; and it does not provide any protection against COVID-19. Alcohol has a deleterious effect on the immune system and does not stimulate immunity or viral resistance at all (Alcohol and COVID-19, n.d.). These warnings have been mostly overlooked in a flood of other health information and rapidly changing epidemiological measures. Therefore, people drew from the memory of folk medicine and from the domestic practice of making alcoholic liquors, different "healing" mixtures.

They actually believed that alcohol (ethanol, e.g., vodka, rum, or homemade Schnaps) combined with some herbs or plants (ginger, garlic, sage, and citrus) would kill the coronavirus, and they prepared special "preventive" mixtures at home and shared recipes online. But, of course, the disinfection happens outside the body, not inside. Drinking 60% liquor will not cure anyone of COVID-19 if the SARS-COV-2 virus is already in the body. Nor does inhaling it cure the disease. It would bypass the liver. It would take a first pass of the alcohol directly to the brain and affect it negatively. Others, in their ignorance and the pervasive emphasis on disinfection, equated all types of alcohol in the first wave and drank disinfectant (rubbing alcohol or isopropyl alcohol) or bleach, not without serious consequences.

It is not possible to say how many alcohol-related injuries or deaths occurred during the pandemic, but the World Health Organization was aware of a number of reported alcohol poisonings associated with COVID-19 that were the result of false claims that consuming alcohol kills the new coronavirus. These claims had no basis in fact, and consumption of high-strength alcohol (ethanol) can cause serious harm and even death. Some of the reported poisonings were caused by methanol added to the products. Methanol is a highly toxic type of alcohol and even in small amounts can cause blindness, kidney failure, and death if ingested. Such poisoning can only occur with industrially produced methanol that has been added to the product. In addition, there have been media reports that incidents of family and domestic violence have increased during the pandemic. There is strong evidence that alcohol consumption is a major contributor to this trend, and community health authorities and police need to be alert to threats to women and children while the pandemic continues (Frequently, 2020: 3–4).

So, in April 2020, one American read somewhere on the Internet that alcohol disinfects the SARS-CoV-2 virus and that it burns a little on the way down but kills the virus. In his mind, the benefits of self-disinfection outweighed that burn and he drank an entire bottle of 91% rubbing alcohol because he feared he had become infected after touching his face at the grocery store. His mother found him unconscious on the floor after he became dizzy, the floor began to spin and he collapsed. Rubbing alcohol entered his liver where it was broken down to acetone. With supportive care at the hospital, he woke up from the coma and was sent home a day later. In other news, people in Iran were reported to be drinking industrial strength alcohol (methanol), which turns into formaldehyde in the body. This chemical was used to embalm mummies. Formaldehyde is a disinfectant, but it is also a poison that causes blindness and stops the heart. Some others drank household bleach (sodium hypochlorite) believing it would cure them of the virus and got severe burns and dead tissue in the inner lining of the esophagus (Bernard, 2020).

A review of thousands of visual and textual memes that circulated during the pandemic also points to vulnerable groups and false claims when it comes to alcohol consumption. Many memes referred to women/mothers seeking solace in alcohol in their overworked work-from-home and long-distance lives. Memes like "Moms during quarantine: Week 2," "Need more wine," "They are never going back to school," "Starting my fruit juice diet: Bottoms up!", "One glass of wine a day keeps a doctor away," "Let's go wine tasting on the couch," "Day 51 of being quarantined with your husband," and others seemed pretty harmless, but the quarantine drinking culture has become problematic because relaxing, relieving social anxiety, not dealing with the hard stuff, or drinking for no reason are pathways to alcoholism per se. Other memes mocked work-from-home outfit or masking, hand-washing, physical distance, and other quarantine and isolation situations. Humor offered some solace in uncertain times, and finding solace in drinking alcohol and even making fun of it became quite normal (See Fig. 11.3). Normalizing alcohol consumption is, of course, one of the alcohol industry's main interests.

These examples suggest that no one has taken seriously the World Health Organization's materials to counter misinformation and provide guidance to individuals and countries during the pandemic, which includes answers to a number of frequently asked questions about alcohol and COVID-19 (Frequently, 2020). In addition, due to the lack of regulation and restrictions on the delivery of alcohol online or to the home, new forms of drinking have developed, such as online wine tasting, online alcohol games, LGBTQIA+ wine parades. All this was also accompanied, under the guise of humor, by a series of memes that sought to normalize or minimize the consequences of drinking.

The World Health Organization suggested that government action was needed to reduce alcohol consumption during the pandemic COVID-19 (Frequently, 2020). It had clearly warned that alcohol products should not be declared or considered "essential items" and the provision of alcohol should not be designated as an "essential service" to be provided online or offline during the pandemic. Alcohol is not an ordinary commodity—it is a psychoactive substance. With millions of people living with high levels of stress and anxiety, isolating themselves, and working from home, everyone should be aware that being kept under lockdown with such a harmful substance carries certain risks. For governments, this means both that additional measures are needed and that existing regulations should be tightened (Frequently, 2020: 3).

The World Health Organization has an extensive portfolio of recommended interventions to reduce alcohol consumption and alcohol-related harm. The best ways to reduce the total amount of alcohol consumed in society are: (1) increasing excise taxes on alcohol to cover the cost of alcohol to society; (2) restricting access to alcoholic beverages at retail—for example, by banning alcohol sales online and home delivery; and (3) introducing comprehensive bans on alcohol advertising, promotion, and sponsorship. These types of interventions are considered by the World Health Organization to be the three best interventions to reduce alcohol-related exposure because they are cost-effective and easy to implement. For this reason, it is advisable to restrict alcohol sales during the pandemic—for example, by reducing the amount a person can buy at one time, limiting the hours of sale, and banning home deliveries and alcohol sales over the internet where proper age verification is not possible. Increased monitoring of illicit alcohol production and sales is necessary to prevent intoxication incidents, and depending on the context, increased enforcement measures and harsher penalties may also be necessary. In addition, governments may consider specific prevention campaigns on the risks of alcohol consumption during the pandemic COVID-19, which could be targeted

Fig. 11.3 Selection of Coronavirus drinking memes of unknown origin, circulating on Facebook and other social media between March 2020 and August 2021, mocking the situation in which we played many roles, including homeschooling children, self-medicating and cheering ourselves, and waiting for the vaccine. Alcohol was present in all of the cases and the memes made fun of people's inability to live without it. Alcohol coronavirus memes were unhelpful coping strategy for dealing with life in isolation, as they attempted to reduce, trivialize, and downplay the harm caused by addiction. Source: Unknown origin memes that have been spreading on Facebook, Pinterest, and group chats since the beginning of the pandemic

(by age, sex, profession, etc.) to different population groups. Finally, competent authorities should develop specific codes and apply appropriate control mechanisms to require the removal of misinformation, especially on social media, where appropriate, as disinformation or fake news about alcohol and COVID-19 is dangerous and has already led to deaths (Frequently, 2020: 3).

The World Health Organization had early indications that online alcohol advertising had increased dramatically in some countries following the introduction of strict home isolation and quarantine measures. There was also evidence that alcohol was being heavily promoted through special offers and deals at outlets and online, while some countries had changed their legislation to allow online alcohol sales and delivery services. The World Health Organization warned that governments should consider restricting this form of advertising specifically to protect citizens, particularly children and adolescents, as exposure to alcohol advertising has been shown to influence their drinking behavior (Frequently, 2020: 3).

Here, we must mention the compromise prizes for those willing to be vaccinated or other strategically not so well-conceived campaigns to lure people to mobile vaccination centers, such as at beer festivals when interest in vaccination began to wane in April and May 2021. These prizes included alcohol-related vaccination incentives, especially free beer at bars and breweries or soft drinks, in addition to lottery prizes, monetary incentives, raffles for a car, tuition for public schools, various fried treats (donuts), prepaid grocery cards, free marijuana joints where it was legal for recreational use, fishing and hunting licenses, tickets to sporting events, free subway weekly passes, raffles for cruises, money for a date with the partner, free state parking passes, free annual memberships to public theaters, and others. Public health trade-offs with subtly sent messages, left many public health workers feeling uneasy and publicly questioning whether the health effects of alcohol consumption were really worth the trade-off for increased vaccination rates. Nonetheless, in a handful of the United States, vaccination incentive programs increased local vaccination rates in some demographics; for example, men were more likely to sign up for vaccination than women. Even when "Shot and a Beer" promotions had people lining up outside the brewery to get their free beer and proudly waving their vaccination cards, the early enthusiasm did not lead to a huge increase in vaccination rates.

Finally, the Portuguese wine industry sought to restore the sense of smell in COVID-19 patients by collaborating with the University of Aveiro to develop a clever sensory kit to retrain the sense of smell in patients with COVID-19 (Neish, 2021). Clinical trials were conducted in a hospital to evaluate the kit's efficiency in regenerating the olfactory epithelium in patients with confirmed loss of sense of smell. The kit contains Portuguese raw materials such as rosemary powder, tangerine peel, pomace powder from local grapes, anise seed, ginger powder, and oregano leaves. The ingredients were chosen for their sustainability as natural resources and the fact that the Portuguese population is familiar with them, which increases the likelihood that smelling them will trigger positive olfactory memories. The Portuguese wine producer supplied the plant material included in the kit and contributed its considerable expertise in aroma analysis. The kit will benefit the wine industry, which has an inseparable relationship with the sense of smell. Wine lovers and those who work in the wine industry, such as sommeliers, and other professions such as chefs and perfumers may also find it useful and should benefit. The kit was developed to be commercially successful in the future (Neish, 2021).

References

Alcohol and COVID-19: what you need to know. (n.d.). *World Health Organization*. Retrieved August 24, 2021 from https://www.euro.who.int/__data/assets/pdf_file/0010/437608/Alcohol-and-COVID-19-what-you-need-to-know.pdf

Alcohol.org. (2020). *Drinking alcohol when working from home*. Retrieved August 24, 2021 from https://www.alcohol.org/guides/work-from-home-drinking/

Bernard. (2020, 22 April). A man drank a bottle of rubbing alcohol for COVID-19. *MedPage Today*. Retrieved August 24, 2021 from https://www.medpagetoday.com/infectiousdisease/covid19/86094

Chesler, C. (2020, 2 April). As pandemic and stay-at-home orders spread, so does alcohol consumption. *The Washington Post*. Retrieved August 24, 2021 from https://www.washingtonpost.com/national/health-science/as-pandemic-and-stay-at-home-orders-spread-so-does-alcohol-consumption/2020/04/02/ad41bc3c-7430-11ea-87da-77a8136c1a6d_story.html

Ferreira, V. (2020, 31 January). Corona beer vs. coronavirus: Why 'doing nothing' about flurry of absurd memes connecting the two may be Constellation's best bet. *Financial Post*. Retrieved August 24, 2021 from https://financialpost.com/news/retail-marketing/corona-beer-vs-coronavirus-why-doing-nothing-about-flurry-of-absurd-memes-connecting-the-two-may-be-constellations-best-bet

Fontaine, M. (2020, 18 April). Ancient advice for drinking at home during coronavirus self-quarantine. *USA Today*. Retrieved August 24, 2021 from https://eu.usatoday.com/story/opinion/2020/04/18/ancient-advice-for-drinking-home-during-coronavirus-self-quarantine-column/5132676002/

Frequently asked questions about alcohol and COVID-19. (2020). World Health Organization. Retrieved August 24, 2021 from https://www.euro.who.int/__data/assets/pdf_file/0007/442690/FAQ-COVID-19-alcohol.pdf

Gibson, M. (2021). How technology is reshaping the liquor industry. *FasTrax*. Retrieved August 24, 2021 from https://www.goftx.com/blogs/posts/how-technology-is-reshaping-the-liquor-industry

Lorch, W. (2020, 28 March). Wine communication goes online. *Wine-Searcher*. Retrieved August 24, 2021 from https://www.wine-searcher.com/m/2020/03/wine-communication-goes-online

Mertes, A. (2021, 27 May). 31 Funny wine glass sayings that everyone is sure to love. *Quality Logo Products Blog*. Retrieved August 24, 2021 from https://www.qualitylogoproducts.com/blog/funny-wine-glass-sayings/

Mileham, A. (2021, 23 June). Bridge: Taylor's expects to sell 1m Portonic cans in first year after strong demand. *The Drinks Business*. Retrieved August 24, 2021 from https://www.thedrinksbusiness.com/2021/06/bridge-taylors-expects-to-sell-1m-portonic-cans-in-first-year/

Mobley, E. (2021, 27 March). Pandemic drinking shows America's all-or-nothing attitude toward alcohol: binge or be sober. *San Francisco Chronicle*. Retrieved August 24, 2021 from https://www.sfchronicle.com/food/wine/article/Pandemic-alcohol-drinking-America-temperance-binge-16030912.php

Morris, R. (2021 9 August). American Gen Z are thoughtful boozers, survey says. *The Drinks Business*. Retrieved August 24, 2021 from https://www.thedrinksbusiness.com/2021/08/american-gen-z-are-thoughtful-boozers-survey-says/

NBC. (2020, 1 April). Study: Alcohol sales on the rise as people stay home. Retrieved August 24 2021 from https://www.nbcmiami.com/news/coronavirus/study-alcohol-sales-on-the-rise-as-people-stay-home/2213998/

Neish, S. (2021, 15 July). Portuguese producer Sogrape co-develops kit to restore sense of smell in Covid patients. *The Drinks Business*. Retrieved August 24, 2021 from https://www.thedrinksbusiness.com/2021/07/portuguese-producer-sogrape-co-develops-kit-to-restore-sense-of-smell-in-covid-patients/

Nilsson, C., Ridoff, N., Szolnoki, G., Tafel, M. & Blaß, M. (2021, 18 May). *Online wine tastings. Wine tourism worldwide – a global survey*. Stockholm, WineTourism and Geisenheim, Geisenheim University. Retrieved August 24 2021 from https://www.winetourism.com/wp-content/uploads/2021/03/OWT_Report_GeisenheimUni_WineTourismCom.pdf

Romano, A. (2021, 15 July). Is canned wine growing up? *Wine Spectator*. Retrieved August 24, 2021 from https://www.winespectator.com/articles/is-canned-wine-growing-up?fbclid=IwAR1GW1_xUy_9R37Ajtz8N4eKqb1mZLkmDImVZThPnuZzZXTpRK_tQKBaNN0

Slaughter T. (2021, 11 April). *Our rules for zoom room drinking game, because why not? the manual*. Retrieved August 24, 2021 from https://www.themanual.com/food-and-drink/zoom-room-drinking-game-rules/

Smith, C. (2021, 4 June). The 10 most valuable beer brands in the world. *The drinks business*. Retrieved August 24, 2021 from https://thedrinksbusiness.com/2021/06/the-10-most-valuable-beer-brands-in-the-world/

Thompson, K. (2020, 4 April). 8 Drinking Games You Can Play with Friends Virtually. *Thrillist*. Retrieved August 24, 2021 from https://www.thrillist.com/drink/nation/online-drinking-games-virtual-happy-hour-activities

Williams, M (2019, 28 August). Is the future of wine in the can? *Forbes*. Retrieved August 24, 2021 from https://www.forbes.com/sites/michellewilliams/2019/08/28/is-the-future-of-wine-in-the-can/?sh=3b8076ed6cc3

Williams, H. A., Williams, R., & Bauman, M. (2018). *Growth of the wine-in-a-can market*. Texas Tech University, College of Human Sciences, Texas Wine Marketing Research Institute. Retrieved August 24, 2021 from https://www.depts.ttu.edu/hs/texaswine/docs/Wine_in_Can_Industry_Report.pdf

14 Zoom Drinking Games to Play Online in 2021 (2021, 21 May). *Teambuilding*. Retrieved August 24 2021 from https://teambuilding.com/blog/zoom-drinking-games

Chapter 12
Femininity, Online Practices of Drinking and Women in Alcohol Industry

> *I have a question. Is it okay to drink while you're pregnant…if you're planning on giving the baby up for adoption?*
>
> *Chelsea Handler,* My Horizontal Life: A Collection of One-Night Stands

Abstract This chapter looks at how shifting societal norms have influenced women's drinking habits and rituals, particularly as young women's drinking becomes more acceptable and even encouraged. Moral concerns about decency, femininity, and safety, as well as social concerns about young women drinking, continue to exist. As a result of the relaxation of rules limiting expected conduct of women, women have become the target of an alcohol industry that targets their hyperfemininity, newly acquired socioeconomic power, and wine knowledge. Women must balance respectability, decorum, and a particular kind of acceptable femininity, exhibited in physical and online hypersexuality or hyperfemininity. Drinking by women happens in public places and is facilitated by social networking sites, as marketers know the potential of social media advertising, which appeals to women.

For much of the twentieth century, drinking by women was frowned upon and considered unfeminine. With the rise of second-wave feminism in the 1960s to 1970s, as women's rights and roles began to change, new opportunities for public drinking opened up for young women as well. Women's social status has changed over time, allowing them greater access to employment and leisure activities that were traditionally considered the domain of men, including drinking. There is no longer a strict spatial demarcation between women's and men's drinking spaces (except perhaps in rural areas), although a spatial element to women's drinking remains. Young women's drinking is now accepted and even encouraged in the twenty-first century, but social anxieties about young women drinking in public persist and there are ongoing moral panics about decency, femininity, and safety. It

M. Ramšak, *Social Impact of Wine Marketing*, Contributions to Management Science, https://doi.org/10.1007/978-3-030-89224-1_12

is important to trace women's historical relationship with alcohol consumption as it shows that women's drinking is always relational—it has always been set against men's drinking and within a patriarchal framework. Young women's drinking takes place in physical space and is reinforced through social networking sites—through the organization of going out, the uploading and sharing of photos, the telling and retelling of drinking stories, and alcohol marketing. Social networking sites provide a new and expanded public drinking space that weaves together online and offline experiences to provide a platform for fun, social belonging, and identity curation. The changing spatiality and temporality of young women's drinking have implications for identity construction and gender relations, most clearly in understandings of femininity. The enactment of femininity and consumption now spans physical and virtual space. Young women use social networking sites more frequently and in different ways than young men. Even within the context of changing gender relations, the ways in which women present themselves in physical and online spaces are subject to moral censorship. Social anxieties about appropriate behavior for young women are nothing new (Lindsay & Supski, 2017: 49, 50).

Young women have become a new target market for the alcohol industry in the night-time economy, and they now have more opportunities to drink and consequently drink more alcohol. The transformation of the night-time economy includes changes in alcohol advertising, marketing, and retailing, as well as opening up female-friendly spaces for young women to drink. Young women can now actively participate in the night-time economy: Their consumption and frequency of going out have increased, as has the strength and type of drinks they consume. With the development of the night-time economy, alcohol has once again become the drug of choice for young people. There is now an everydayness associated with young people's alcohol consumption that has become an almost obligatory aspect of young people's lives. Multinational alcohol companies have followed the new market of young women and created new fashion drinks for them, especially with white spirits, and marketed the products heavily both online and offline to a young female audience (Lindsay & Supski, 2017: 50, 51).

Women must navigate the tension between maintaining the patriarchal understanding of femininity, which includes respectability, propriety, and desirability, and a certain kind of acceptable femininity, manifested by being hypersexual or hyperfeminine in physical and online space (i.e., always stylishly groomed but not too flashy, youthful, sassy, high heels, short skirts, low cut tops, fake tan, long straight hair, smooth bare legs in all climates, lots of makeup, slim, and sexually knowledgeable while drunk and having fun). Hypersexuality is also a potential problem. Young women have to negotiate conflicting desires when going out—having fun and enjoying being with friends while avoiding potential risks associated with excessive drinking and drunkenness (Lindsay & Supski, 2017: 53, 54, 55, 57, 58).

Hyperfemininity is also one of the drives of lifestyle marketing, where certain types of lifestyle activities are identity-provoking and where both lifestyle and identity can be fused in the decision to purchase items that reflect a desired lifestyle. Lifestyle is an important psychographic category composed of a combination of factors such as activities, interests, and opinions. The status value of purchase appeals to consumers who seek to create a personal identity through consumption, and their spending behavior is based on lifestyle and personal identity. In this type of conspicuous consumption, the individual acquires status not only in the eyes of others but also in their own eyes, which is reinforced by a desired lifestyle (Michman & Mazze, 2006: 45, 116). A special case of hyperfeminine drinkers is promotional girls who participate in a marketing event. They are valuable when it comes to increasing a company's brand awareness. They can boost business by acting as spokespeople as they know the local market well, create better customer response and a lively atmosphere, and are an asset to the brand. Therefore, another form of wine marketing guerrilla emerged, using real characters whose lifestyle also appeals to drinkers, such as wine queens (Ramšak, 2015). Wine queens and, more rarely, wine kings promote wines and viticulture with their appearance (queens) or knowledge and economic success (kings) and spread the culture of wine drinking. However, wine queens are not only promoters of sophisticated wine drinking, but also mascots in the service of the wine industry, which uses this market niche to attract new, younger consumers. The sophisticated appearance of the wine queen is a visual metaphor as it creates an analogy between the shape of a wine bottle and the shape of a woman's body (Negro, 2015: 126), thus illustrating the essential visual characteristics of a bottle with similar female figure features. The fashion, cosmetics, and sports industries are also making inroads into wine marketing here. Since every wine queen, whether national, regional, or local, has a social media profile with many followers, winemakers can gain inordinately more attention through their figure than if they were only marketing the product of their labor, wine. Wine queens are a reference group with whom other single girls like to compare themselves in activities, interests, and opinions. At promotional events such as wine festivals, tastings, pruning, grape harvesting, and the like, the visual and behavioral example of the wine queens is followed by many other girls who covertly or openly sympathize with the idea of wine promoters. Their body techniques suggest a decent femininity that does not cross the line of self-control when drinking, their appearance suggests that they are fashion conscious, their behavior that they are sensitive to social status and that they have plenty of free time. Of course, they do not forget to mark their presence on social media or pose for the posts of others present. This is an example of why lifestyle marketing is so successful. Imitators of other people's lifestyles unintentionally, unreservedly, and for free advertise what they identify with. Wine queens are a niche advantage for smaller wine producers competing with stronger companies in a highly competitive wine market. This niche is customer focused, observing trends, trying to satisfy tastes and desires as opposed to the needs of specific target groups.

There is also another type of advertising girls, who are a brutal example of the use of young women to increase beer sales in Heineken's marketing strategy in ten African countries (van Breemen, 2019). They are subjected to unwanted intimacies, forced to allow groping, forced to sleep with managers, sexual acts are part of their job. Some of these girls are also prostitutes, and they use beer solicitation to get in touch with customers. They are also forced to drink five to ten bottles of beer every working day to persuade customers to consume more. They earn crumbs and have to pay all additional medical expenses—especially for gynecologists and abortion clinics—themselves. The alarm was first raised in 2010 by a report by the humanitarian organization, which found that more than half of Heineken's advertising girls in Cambodia were sexually harassed, 90% were sexually intimidated and 20% were infected with HIV. According to the report, it was normal for customers to reach under the women's skirts and touch their breasts. Almost no one cared about the promotional girls. Later improvements were made in some countries, but headquarters dropped the issue and no longer monitors it. Heineken still relies on young women using their bodies to boost beer sales. The sexualization of beer is a marketing strategy that reinforces the idea that beer drinking is a male, heterosexual activity. Beer girls hired by bar owners to walk around the premises and encourage men to drink are also a well-known phenomenon in Asia. Heineken promised to investigate the beer girl problem, stating that it was completely against what they stood for as a company and strongly condemned these abuses—but did nothing, only finding the excuse that the beer promoters were not employed by Heineken but through outside agencies, making it difficult to properly monitor their working conditions. News of the hundreds of Heineken beer girls prompted the Global Fund to Fight AIDS, tuberculosis, and malaria to suspend its partnership with Heineken, launched in 2018, because the company employs female beer promoters in ways that expose them to sexual exploitation and health risks (van Breemen, 2019).

Misogynistic and sexist behavior in the beer and craft beer industry is rampant. In 2021, after a brewery owner asked Instagram users to share their experiences of sexism and harassment in the workplace, more than 1000 detailed, harrowing incidents of sexual harassment, assault, and racism by owners and supervisors toward women working at various breweries surfaced, forcing beer companies across the United States to issue apologies and resignations. The women told of being assaulted in the workplace, groped by strangers and co-workers, belittled by supervisors, treated as inferior in their own company, and made to feel like they did not belong. Brewer became an amplifier, sharing the anonymous stories publicly, forwarding messages to brewers and asking business owners if they knew this was happening and what they were doing about it (Guerra, 2021). The avalanche of stories like those shared on Instagram and Twitter, along with reports showing that 60% of women working in the hospitality industry in the United States have experienced sexual violence in their workplace, show that the dangers women perceive as commonplace are often completely unknown to men, and that they are exempt from them—if they are not complicit in committing them or silent if they witness them (Demmon, 2021). Later, a new Instagram account was also managed by volunteers to handle the volume of stories shared. The wave of solidarity through fundraising and hosting craft brew nights to discuss sexism and racism began and joined an organization Pink Boots Society that supports and empowers female brewers. The issue has become unmissable and if craft beer is serious about making a difference for the future, it is now up to men to overcome their misogyny, hold their peers to account and work to make the industry a safer place for all (Guerra, 2021; Demmon, 2021).

Similarly, LGBTQIA+ members working in the wine industry report receiving many offensive comments from customers and being asked questions that put them in a very uncomfortable position (Bennett, 2021). For example, they get very personal questions in the professional setting of tasting rooms or direct offers to date customers' sons, even if they do not want to have that conversation. On several occasions, they have heard customers who have very conservative political or religious beliefs point to the employee's wedding ring and ask about her husband. They are often faced with odd moments where they are unsure if it is safe to come out because the idea of revealing something personal feels risky and scary. They also often experience weird or uncomfortable micro-aggressions from people in the workplace, such as uncomfortable jokes, objectification, and belittling of women. Women face multiple challenges because of their intersectionality—being both female and queer in an industry where neither is common. Queer men also have their own challenges due to societal definitions and expectations of masculinity, especially in certain parts of the wine industry. They fear not being accepted and/or seen as competent if they are compared to a straight man because some production workers believe that a gay man cannot drive a forklift, operate barrels, or perform other manual tasks as well as a straight man. Even though they do not fear for their personal safety as much as women do, they worry about losing respect. LGBTQIA+ people are therefore subject to a lot of micro-aggressions—mainly because people's lips loosen up after a few drinks (Bennett, 2021).

For trans people, it is even more difficult and there are many more concerns and worries because emotional and physical violence against trans people is even more common. And if people have consumed alcohol, then it becomes dangerous. There is a real concern about safety. Trans men who work in tasting rooms avoid standing out, for example, they do not wear nail polish or do anything else that might go against gender norms (Bennett, 2021).

In 2020, when the first Oregon Wine Country Pride Parade was organized for the first time and videos of the event were included in the winery newsletter, there was some very unpleasant feedback online (Bennett, 2021). The wine industry seemed to support LGBTQIA+ rights during the pandemic because there was an opportunity to make more money. There is also, of course, the difference between consumerism that tokenizes LGBTQIA+ people for profit and activism.

Aside from reviewing their internal culture and finding ways to give to minority communities without asking for more in return, there are many things the wine industry can do to become more inclusive and welcoming to people under the LGBTQIA+ umbrella. One of the most important things is to provide more training and education for employees. Queer employees need to know that they have management's support when they stand up to customers who behave in offensive ways. Companies also need to make sure employees know and trust that the employer has their back if they are openly gay, and create an environment that is accepting and inclusive and holds those who do not adhere to these values accountable. There are numerous other things wineries can do to support the queer community, such as seeking health insurance policies that cover medical issues specific to the LGBTQIA+ community, including transgender healthcare. Tasting rooms can designate restrooms as gender neutral, have better representation in the media, including in advertising—wine ads showing a gay couple at the dinner table instead of a straight couple, which is already normal in the beer and spirits industry. These things are important from a moral perspective, but there is also an economic reason for them. Owners who take responsibility for diversifying their businesses and making sure they are welcoming and inclusive are likely to experience higher sales and broader support (Bennett, 2021).

The trend away from sexualizing women to sell alcohol to men to alcohol brands attempting to align their products with sophistication, female power, and female friendship is accompanied by slogans that highlight women's accomplishments in a patronizing way (e.g., "you've come a long way, baby"). The trend toward women-focused marketing is not surprising given the rise in women's socioeconomic power. This has led to the emergence of numerous new alcohol products aimed at female customers, from fruit-flavored beers to low-calorie drinks with a focus on slimness, weight, pink packaging, glitter, messages of sisterhood, female friendships, motherhood, and even the perennial favorite, sexiness (See Fig. 12.1). Messages of empowerment have increased, as has the celebration of women—for example, in conjunction with International Women's Day, Valentine's Day, and even Mother's Day (The Feminisation, 2020).

Social networking sites have indeed become new public spaces for women to display, create, and maintain their female identities and friendships. For young women, the connection between showing photos and alcohol is a feminine activity. The airbrushed effect of photos associated with going out and drinking serves to reinforce the acceptance of certain drinking habits. Only certain drinking photos are posted. Airbrushing the negative aspects of young people's drinking normalizes and reinforces drinking as an always enjoyable behavior with no harmful consequences. Facebook's wall feature serves as a place where users and their friends can actively shape their online identities. The importance of self- and other-generated identity construction on social networking sites is particularly important in the context of young women's drinking, as young women actively curate their online selves. They choose, edit and post photos that show how their identities clash with the new drinking culture on offer to them—often portraying themselves as drunk, messy, rowdy, but also as confident, strong, and sexy young women. They curate their online selves to show their commitment to drinking and fun nights out, but they also actively edit their photos to minimize the appearance of drunkenness to both known and unknown viewers. One way they curate their identities is by removing themselves from photos posted by friends or others. Young women actively check their friends' Facebook pages and remove their names from photos that show them in a derogatory light, such as heavily intoxicated or compromising. This curation and construction of identity adhere to gendered norms of respectability and femininity, ensuring that the practice of femininity is not labeled as promiscuous or disreputable. Social networking sites like Facebook also cause anxiety because it is challenging to deal with multiple audiences, including family, friends, classmates, and potential and

Fig. 12.1 *Grička vještica* (Croatian), "The Witch of the Hill," dark strong lager brewed since 1996, named after a popular theme from the literature of Marija Jurić, who wrote a cycle of seven historical novels *The Witch of the Hill.* This is an example of a strong beer produced in small batches in an independent brewery that used Myth-making and cultural memory with a theme of discrimination of women to appeal to female customers. Source: Photo Mojca Ramšak, September 2019

current employers. Anxious politics is particularly evident in the regular moral panics around young women and alcohol use (Lindsay & Supski, 2017: 55–58).

The marketing of alcohol to certain groups can have disturbing consequences. The impact of alcohol marketing on mothers is one area of concern. Feminized marketing has popularized terms like "mummy juice" and "wine o'clock" and links them to the way busy women deal with anxiety. This means that women are using alcohol as an acceptable form of self-medication and stress relief, as a kind of reward at the end of the day. Social media is a big driver of female alcohol consumption by creating unhealthy habits. Many women are at risk of sliding down the alcohol use disorder scale, especially if they drink in the ways promoted by social media posts, T-shirts, or similar products (The Feminisation, 2020).

Efforts to expand the female market for alcohol have certainly worked, as women now drink almost as much as their male counterparts and alcohol abuse among women is on the rise. This trend is most evident among young adults (The Feminisation, 2020; Bratberg et al., 2016). When children absorb messages aimed at adults, this can also have potential consequences later in life, as alcohol advertising normalizes alcohol consumption and young people consume the same media and absorb the same alcohol messages as adults. Policy changes should limit alcohol advertising and better regulate the types of messages that reach young girls in particular. This can curb some of the damage that feminized marketing can do, both online and in broadcast media, and support organizations that promote alcohol-free lifestyles. The "DontPinkMyDrink" Tweeter campaign launched in 2019, which asked women to tweet examples of products that equate female drinking with pink, with fun, with friendship, with empowerment, highlighted the ways companies use condescending tropes to appeal to women: cotton candy-colored labels, sweet flavors, low-calorie products, suggestions that it is "wine o'clock," or Johnnie Walker, which turns its male mascot into a female version, Jane. Gendered marketing continues to be a reality in all aspects of daily life, and the alcohol industry is happy to jump on the marketing bandwagon and use feminism to increase its profits. In the past, it had launched misguided products specifically for International Women's Day and these cynical moves to appeal to women were widely criticized. Unleashing many of the values that these alcohol ads and products tap into—happiness, independence, self-determination—will take real change. An advertised bottle of overpriced rosé does not really challenge deep structural inequalities, because feeling empowered is not the same as actually being empowered (#DontPinkMyDrink, 2019; The Feminisation, 2020).

Alcohol industry-funded organizations were statistically significantly less likely to provide information about fetal alcohol spectrum disorders than public health websites and less likely to advise that no amount of alcohol is safe during pregnancy (Lim et al., 2019). They were significantly more likely to emphasize uncertainty and less likely to use direct language (e.g., "don't drink"). Some alcohol industry-funded (rather than public health funded) websites appear to use "alternative causation" arguments (e.g., proposing alternative, non-alcohol causes of harm in pregnancy), much like the tobacco industry, to argue other causes of alcohol harm in pregnancy or to present the evidence as a matter of opinion or belief, and that "light" or "moderate" drinking is equivalent to abstinence. Alcohol industry-funded websites omit and misrepresent the evidence for the main risks of alcohol use in pregnancy. This may mislead women to continue drinking during pregnancy. These findings suggest that alcohol industry-funded sites may increase the risk to pregnant women by spreading misinformation. Misrepresentation of the harmful effects of alcohol during pregnancy may be a broader industry strategy involving the highlighting of uncertainty and the use of ambiguous contexts and language to reduce the impact of, or distract from, information about harmful effects (which may be accurate in itself). It may also involve distracting from the independent risks of alcohol consumption by highlighting non-modifiable potential confounders and undermining scientific evidence by emphasizing "balance" and "debate" and presenting scientific evidence as "beliefs." The same approach has already been documented in relation to alcohol and cancer risk, and there are many examples from the tobacco industry and other industries over many decades. Therefore, the public should be made fully aware of the risks associated with receiving health information from alcohol industry-funded sources (Lim et al., 2019).

Because of such relativization of the harmfulness of alcohol to pregnant women and the fetus, the alcohol industry offers a number of "substitute" products from the category of low-alcohol beverages. The trend is mainly towards hybrid alcoholic drinks with 0.5% alcohol, e.g., made from gin or rum, with sugar or sugar-free with and aromatic additives and cocktail mixes with champagne, rosé, flavored wines, or flavored beer. The alcohol industry tries to woo female consumers with drinks in ladylike colors (pink, peach, light blue, yellow), ultra-feminine packaging, alternatively unisex packaging, or other girly features. What the alcohol industry is trying to do is impose a state of mind, lifestyle, or way of life on female drinkers, even if they are pregnant, to see the world through the rose-colored glasses of alcohol intoxication. What seems like a nice invitation to indulge in sophistication and good taste is a ploy and cunning abuse aimed at creating a lifelong drinker. Alcohol abstinence in pregnant women without pretty pink sips and hash-tagged cravings isn't perfectly Instagrammable, of course.

References

Bennett, S. (2021, 16 June). A look at LBGTQIA+ Issues in wine, and how the industry can solve them. *VinePair*. Retrieved August 24, 2021 from https://vinepair.com/articles/wine-industry-lgbtqia-community/

Bratberg, G. H., Wilsnack, S. C., Wilsnack, R., Håvås, H. S., Krokstad, S., Reidar, S. E. & Haakon, B. J. (2016). Gender differences and gender convergence in alcohol use over the past three decades (1984–2008), the HUNT study, Norway. *BMC Public Health*, *16*, 723. Retrieved August 24, 2021 from https://www.ncbi.nlm.nih.gov/pmc/articles/PMC4974746/

van Breemen, O. (2019). *Heineken in Africa: A multinational unleashed.* Hurst and Company.

Demmon, B. (2021, 10 May). Buzz Kill — The physical, psychological, and financial price women pay for working in beer. Retrieved August 24, 2021 from https://www.goodbeerhunting.com/blog/2021/5/19/buzz-kill-the-physical-psychological-and-financial-price-women-pay-for-working-in-beer

#DontPinkMyDrink. (2019). *Alcohol focus Scotland.* Retrieved August 24, 2021 from https://www.alcohol-focus-scotland.org.uk/campaigns-policy/alcohol-marketing/dontpinkmydrink/

Guerra, C. (2021, 27 May). How a mass. Brewers call for harassment stories led to a reckoning in the beer industry. *The ARTery*. Retrieved August 24, 2021 from https://www.wbur.org/artery/2021/05/27/women-in-beer-industry-harassment-speak-out

Lim, A. W. Y., Van Schalkwyk, M. C. I., Maani, H. N., & Petticrew, M. P. (2019). Pregnancy, fertility, breastfeeding, and alcohol consumption: An analysis of framing and completeness of information disseminated by alcohol industry-funded organizations. *Journal of Studies on*

Alcohol and Drugs, 80(5), 524–533. Retrieved August 24, 2021 from https://www.jsad.com/doi/10.15288/jsad.2019.80.524

Lindsay, J., & Supski, S. (2017). Curating identity. Drinking, young women, femininities and social media practices. In A. C. Lyons, T. McCreanor, I. Goodwin, & H. M. Barnes (Eds.), *Youth drinking cultures in a digital world: Alcohol, social media and cultures of intoxication.* Routledge.

Michman, R. D., & Mazze, E. M. (2006). *The affluent consumer: Marketing and selling the luxury lifestyle*. Praeger Publishers.

Negro, A. I. (2015). Visual wine metaphor and metonymy in ads. Procedia of 32nd International Conference of the Spanish Association of Applied Linguistics (AESLA): Language Industries and Social Change. *Social and Behavioral Sciences* 173, 125–131e.

Ramšak, M. (2015). *Wine Queens: Understanding the role of women in wine marketing*. Springer Briefs in Business.

The Feminisation of alcohol marketing. (2020, 19 September). Woman's Hour. *BBC*. Retrieved August 24, 2021 from https://www.bbc.com/worklife/article/20200924-the-feminisation-of-alcohol-marketing

Chapter 13
Brand Stretching and Popular Culture

The forecast for tonight is alcohol, low standards, and poor decisions.

Laura Kreitzer, Love's Paradox

Abstract The main focus of this chapter is the brand stretching or marketing of alcohol with other things, such as movies, music, sports, reality programs, or people, such as celebrities, in order to persuade customers to buy. Statistics that do not have a favorable impact on young people are presented to the film and music industries when they portray or sing about alcohol and harmful consequences. The alcohol industry hires celebrities for a variety of reasons, including their reputation, the genuineness of their advertising messaging, their use of the drinks they advertise, and their hidden involvement in the alcohol campaign. Their advertising function is now quite comparable to that of social media. Smart product placement is becoming more popular in online advertising, which appeals to younger consumers in particular.

Popular culture has a great influence on people's behavior and decision-making processes. People learn from personal experiences and are influenced by behaviors they observe or perceive in other formats such as movies, television, music, social media, magazines, and advertising. As a result, alcohol brands have several popular culture mediums at their disposal to promote their products and suggest drinking behaviors to potential consumers, especially younger audiences. The portrayal of alcohol consumption in popular culture has led to an unhealthy glorification of alcohol that encourages dangerous drinking habits (Hoeg, 2021). The social aspect of drinking can be used in discrete ways to create social capital (Heath, 2010: 33).

Marketing alcohol with other goods is the trick known as brand stretching, indirect advertising, alibi advertising, co-advertising, or trademark diversification, and has been deliberately developed to circumvent advertising bans. The brand name is infiltrated into popular culture by attaching it to items that have only fantasy

M. Ramšak, *Social Impact of Wine Marketing*, Contributions to Management Science, https://doi.org/10.1007/978-3-030-89224-1_13

associations with the product. Brand stretching has been used primarily with items likely to be used by teenagers, such as alcohol and cigarettes; or advertising alcohol production plants instead of their products with the same brand names (Proctor, 2011: 127, 128).

Product placement, where a company pays a broadcaster TV or programmer to include its products or brands in a program, and native advertising or sponsored content, where advertising is integrated into the platform's native content, are also legally defined.

According to Article 1(1)(m) of the Directive 2010/13/EU of the European Parliament and of the Council of 10 March 2010 on the coordination of certain provisions administered by law, regulation or administrative action in Member States concerning the provision of audiovisual media services (Directive 2010/13/EU) "product placement" refers to any form of audiovisual commercial communication that includes or refers to a product, service, or trademark in order for it to be featured within a program in exchange for payment or similar consideration (Nowak-Gruca, 2018: 39). The "native ad" is a hybrid of subliminal advertising and hidden advertising. It also has something to do with product placement. However, native advertising content—more than other forms of advertising—may be close to information. It is worthwhile to attempt to define the legal boundaries of these concepts. The Directive 2010/13/EU of the European Parliament and of the Council of 10 March 2010 on the coordination of certain provisions administered by law, regulation, or administrative action in Member States concerning the provision of audiovisual media services (Directive 2010/13/EU) should be the first point of reference in the context of native advertising. Furthermore, the Directive 2010/13/EU establishes two important prohibitions in the context of native advertising: one for hidden advertising (Art. 9(1)(a)) and the other for the use of subliminal techniques (Art. 9(1)(b)). Member States and the Commission shall encourage media service providers to develop codes of conduct concerning inappropriate audiovisual commercial communications accompanying or included in children's programs, of foods and beverages containing nutrients and substances with a nutritional or physiological effect, particularly fat, trans-fatty acids, salt/sodium, sugars, or excess sugars (Art. 9) This Directive prohibits product placement (Article 11(2)), with exceptions where such action is permitted (Article 11(3) and (4)) (Nowak-Gruca, 2018: 39-40).

The evidence shows that legal restrictions are more than necessary. For example, a study conducted in 1996 and 2017 found a huge increase in the portrayal of alcohol brands in the top 100 films of the year (Muldoon, 2021). The first go-round found 140 depictions of branded alcohol; 20 years later, that number has risen to 282, a 96% increase. Incidental alcohol consumption refers to films in which characters drink alcohol or otherwise interact with alcohol without alcohol being the focus of the film. Some level of incidental alcohol use is observed in 80% of films. While this type of alcohol consumption may seem harmless, it serves as a promotional tool for alcohol brands. Brands feel safe being featured in movies through product placement, a form of native advertisements. Native advertising describes a type of advertising that intentionally mimics the content in which it appears so as not to break the immersion. Product placement acts as a covert advertisement that does not attract undue attention, but still represents the brand in a film. A character drinking a beer at the bar during a scene could be considered an advertisement if the label on the can is clearly visible. If the character were to pick up the can and deliver a monolog that had nothing to do with the plot, this would not be native advertising. Nearly every genre of film has dealt with the effects of alcoholism from their respective perspectives. This focused examination of the negative aspects of alcohol usually negates any promotional effect that may result from accidental alcohol consumption. The concern that these films show in relation to alcoholism mirrors the concern that researchers have in relation to the potential impact of the rampant portrayal of alcohol in film (Muldoon, 2021).

A 2012 study reveals some worrying patterns in adolescent drinking. A study of 6500 10- to 14-year olds found that those who regularly watched movies that featured alcohol were twice as likely to drink alcohol and three times more likely to binge drink than those who did not. The study points to the learning by example that young people often follow in their development. The frequent appearance of alcohol consumption in films normalizes it and may even portray it as desirable and worthwhile (Muldoon, 2021). Children and teenagers look to movie stars as role models. For alcohol companies, when a favorite star uses a particular brand of alcohol, that brand becomes associated with all the qualities that young admirers see in their movie idol. Therefore, it is not surprising that the brands frequently featured in movies are the most heavily advertised brands and the same brands that underage drinkers tend to drink (Academy of Pediatrics, 2017). The placement of alcohol brands in movies has increased year after year, especially in movies with children's releases. In the first two decades of the twenty-first century, alcohol advertising in movies has almost doubled. It is an effective marketing method, and there is a correlative relationship with the increase in underage and unhealthy drinking habits. The study of American Academy of Pediatrics in 2017, which included 534 films, found that more than half of them contained at least one appearance by an alcohol brand. General alcohol consumption was featured in 87% of all films, while specific brands appeared in only 44%. In movies rated for children, characters drinking alcohol were shown in 85% of all top movies. Alcohol brands appeared in 41%. Moreover, the brands that appeared most frequently in these movies were the preferred, most frequently used brands by underage drinkers. Only three alcohol brands (Budweiser, Miller, and Heineken) accounted for nearly one-third (33%) of all brand placements, with Budweiser appearing in the most child-release films (15%) (American Academy of Pediatrics, 2017; Hoeg, 2021).

Also, in 2016, volunteers in a study watched Hollywood movies in either a 2D, 3D, or 4D version (the 3D movie with added scent). The researchers from three Austrian Universities then recorded the extent to which the volunteers could remember and recognize the brands placed in the movies. They distinguished between prominently and subtly placed products. The results suggest that companies that want to work with less prominent product placement may benefit from continuing to use films created in 2D technology. However, in certain circumstances, the use of 3D films for prominent product placement can be very useful. However, this is only true if the product placement is both highly visible and central to the plot of the film. If this is not the case, 3D technology helps create a negative effect on brand recall and recognition. Regardless of the level of prominence, recall of product placements was poorest for 4D films. The limited information processing capacity of the human brain is responsible for these results. When we watch a 3D or 4D movie, more cognitive resources are required than when we watch a 2D movie. These cognitive resources are then no longer available for processing and memorizing product placements. The additional stimulation in 3D or 4D leads to a more intensive use of the brain (Alpen-Adria-Universität Klagenfurt/Graz/Wien, 2016). According to Drizly, an American e-commerce platform that facilitates the delivery of alcoholic beverages to consumers' homes, 68% of Millennials (those aged 25 to 40) stated celebrity endorsement influenced their purchasing decision, while Generation Z (those born after January 1, 2000) say they do not care. Nearly a third of Gen Z is concerned about minority or ethnic ownership, such as BIPOC (Black, Indigenous and People of Color), women, AAPI (Asian Americans and Pacific Islanders), LGBTQ+, and sustainable business practices, with 40% saying they consider environmental track record when choosing an alcoholic beverage, followed by Gen X, aged 40 to 56 (30%), Millennials (32%), and Baby Boomers, aged 57 to 75 years (20%) respectively (Morris, 2021).

Today's TV program is full of references to alcohol and depictions of drinking. One of the most common forms is product placement—a marketing strategy in which liquor companies pay TV to have their products featured on programs. Another and more recent trend is for television shows to serve as platforms to educate viewers about risky behaviors, including alcohol abuse. However, many of these depictions are solely for entertainment purposes. The top five genres for alcohol portrayal on TV, including commercials aired during the program and the portrayal of alcohol on the air, are: sport, comedy, animated series, reality shows, and drama. It appears that alcohol is almost constantly on screen in the various televised sporting events, commercials, and prime-time shows. The inclusion of alcohol in these shows has been shown to influence viewer drinking behavior, especially among young people (Hilliard, 2021b).

A study conducted by the University of Nottingham analyzed a total of 5129 clips from TV reality shows and found that alcohol was present in 42% of clips and 100% of all full episodes analyzed. Rates of substance use in reality shows are higher than in all other types of prime-time shows—although there are fewer reality shows than scripted series on TV. Another recent study found that 79% of "meals" in non-scripted shows are simply drinks. The same study also found that more female characters in non-scripted shows are portrayed in alcohol-heavy situations than their male counterparts. These findings are concerning because the majority of viewers of reality shows on TV are young women. The constant exposure to drugs that these shows provide is a major factor in young people's alcohol abuse. Researchers argue that excessive alcohol consumption by protagonists is normalized and accepted by viewers because reality shows are more likely to be perceived as credible due to the age and status of the protagonists (Hilliard, 2021b).

Reality shows on television that pit contestants against each other in food service and successful cocktail sales or business and feature well-known media personalities are an example of a powerful alcohol wheel that promotes humiliating and shaming games among contestants in an alcohol-fueled atmosphere. The events show that business is based on attracting young and even the youngest drinkers with: crazy parties with music groups with alcoholic names, alcoholic releases after work (e.g., After-work Gin Party), weekly mid-evening gatherings with sparkling wine, introduction to Octoberfest with special discounts, gatherings with delicious liqueurs on certain days of the week, special prices of booze on and after TV shows, parties in Cuban rhythms with special prices of Bacardi-Cola, charity parties with discounts on vodka cocktails, cocktail evenings, Kiss sensual dance evenings with special alcohol discounts, fashion events with special discounts on alcoholic beverages, stand-up evenings with discounts and—expectedly—with family days and children's corners and workshops, while their parents can "carefree enjoy top-notch coffees." This offer paints a clear picture of the emergence of alcohol dependence, which is promoted as something self-evident and attractive by the alcohol industry in cooperation with commercial media houses. In any case, it is propaganda that is not prohibited by law, as they did not yet exist at the time of the creation and adoption of various anti-alcohol regulations, and so the legislators could not even detect it.

Similarly, today's music is full of allusions to alcohol and often even celebrates excessive drinking as a fun and beneficial activity. A study conducted by Northwestern University found that 22.4% of songs on the Billboard Hot 100 list mention alcohol. Another study by Boston University and Johns Hopkins University examined Billboard's lists of most popular songs from 2009 to 2011 and identified 720 songs, of which a whopping 167 (23.2%) mentioned alcohol. The three genres of music in which alcohol appears most frequently are: Hip-Hop & Rap, Country and Pop. Alcohol use was most frequently addressed in rap and hip-hop music. These genres accounted for 37.7% of songs that mentioned alcohol, and tequila, vodka, cognac, and champagne were mentioned most often. Country music was the second most common genre in which alcohol was mentioned, with 32% of mentions. Pop music was third with 30.5% of mentions. Unlike rap and hip-hop, whiskey and beer were mentioned most often in country and pop music. In the songs of all these genres, alcohol is for the most part portrayed in a positive light, and only rarely are the negative consequences of alcohol consumption mentioned. Many of these songs also specifically target younger audiences and encourage dangerous drinking behaviors (Hilliard, 2021a).

The placement of alcohol brands in song lyrics has essentially become a form of mass marketing that has been shown to have a positive correlation with alcohol sales. A study conducted by the School of Public Health found that Billboard lists of the most popular songs in 2009, 2010 and 2011 featured four liquor brands with surprising frequency: Patron tequila, Hennessy cognac, Grey Goose vodka, and Jack Daniel's whiskey. They accounted for more than half of the brands mentioned in songs that referenced alcohol brands, and most of those references were positive rather than negative. According to the study, the brand names were associated with wealth (63.4%), sex (58.5%), luxury objects (51.2%), parties (48.8%), other drugs (43.9%), and vehicles (39%). Sales of these brands skyrocketed, while the songs in which they were mentioned remained at the top of the charts (Hilliard, 2021a).

Influencer marketing is advertising using influencers. The goal of this advertising is to give the user the impression that the product is also used by a celebrity. There are different types of influencer marketing such as: paid endorsement, product placement, affiliate marketing, free products, invitation to events, and ambassadors. A particular and effective form of alcohol marketing is advertising using film, music, sport and other celebrities, who are paid millions by the alcohol industry to appear publicly alongside a particular brand and talk about its quality. The alcohol industry productively places alcoholic beverages on billboards, on television, in digital media, through music, animated and feature films, uses human brands, i.e., people with some social influence, gives their logos to consumer products (e.g., glasses and paper napkins), organizes product-related trips or excursions, identifies alcohol brands with popular and recognizable places, which works in such a way that the thought of the image of that place is also associated with the wine produced there—and it is ironic that sometimes state and local government tourism institutions join in. All this is due to the ban on direct alcohol advertising.

In all categories where alcohol is promoted through film, music, and celebrities, we can see the glorification or idolization of alcohol in popular culture. Often it is real people, such as politicians or celebrities, who know that association with alcohol will help them gain approval and recognition. There is a common narrative that with the right drink, you can become "somebody." It works the other way around, too. When consumers see professional models on their social media promoting a new alcoholic beverage, the message they get is, "You can be just as beautiful and fit as me if you drink this." On television, most portrayals of alcohol take place in fictional shows. This allows brands and show writers to create worlds where alcohol consumption is associated with a glamorous and affluent lifestyle. In all of these forms of media, the potentially negative consequences of alcohol consumption are not shown. This is, of course, not realistic. However, the real-world effects of this type of marketing in popular culture have led to numerous cases of underage drinking and unhealthy alcohol consumption trends (Hoeg, 2021).

The large exposure to alcohol via bloggers and influencers was found in a 2020 Norwegian study (Influencers, 2021), in a country where alcohol advertising is prohibited. The researchers looked at how alcohol is portrayed and promoted in mediums. They monitored 20 Norwegian influencers over 30 days and gathered data from their Instagram, Snapchat, YouTube, blogs, Facebook, and TikTok accounts. This yielded 13,183 postings, which were used to conduct the analysis. The primary findings were that 329 of the posts depicted alcohol in some way, equating to 11 posts per day and 82 posts per week. That's a total of 3948 posts in a year; 670 saved posts in Instagram highlights included alcohol exposure; 8% of previously published posts had alcohol exposure; 9% of posts with alcohol had a logo and company name; and all posts with alcohol represented alcohol as a positive aspect. Despite the fact that all of the posts in the study were most likely not paid advertising, which would have been unlawful, it is still difficult for the general public to tell what is and is not an advertisement. The findings demonstrate that the general population is exposed to what could be classified as alcohol advertising—

and that the lines between alcohol promotion and freedom of expression are blurry (Influencers, 2021).

If we take the world-renowned sparkling wine as an example, we can follow the evolution of advertising in this case. Marketing techniques for advertising Moët & Chandon champagne have been known since 1866, when champagne companies hired entertainers to sing the praises of the quality of a particular champagne brand, after which they managed to transfer this to literature, art, and later film (Sugarfly, 2017).

These successful marketing methods led to champagne becoming a mandatory part of celebrations and it still remains so today. Champagne advertising marketing techniques have also been successful in conjunction with the film industry, for example, one of the most famous examples is the Dom Pérignon in the 1963 films James Bond, which the protagonist later replaced with the Bollinger, which appeared in twelve films until 1973 (Sugarfly, 2017).

Another example of James Bond's cultural influence is the vodka martini drink from the 1962 film *Dr. No*, based on Ian Fleming's 1958 novel, in which the actor (Sean Connery as a secret agent 007) used the well-known phrase "Shaken, not stirred," which means shaking the drink's ingredients rather than stirring them with a special spoon, which is, by the way, an incorrect way of preparing the drink because shaking muddles the ingredients. In any case, the film had such an impact that in the 1960s and 1970s, consumption of vodka martini and Smirnoff vodka used in the film surged (Kellerman, 2015). "Shaken, not stirred" was James Bond's usual martini order throughout the 007 series, except in the film *You Only Live Twice* (1967), when the host hands him a martini and asks, "Stirred, not shaken?", and Bond says it's fine without batting an eye, clearly forgetting his long-held inclination to the contrary (Rubin, 2021: 1627). James Bond drank a lot of Chianti, Ouzo, Irish Coffee, Mint Juleps (a cocktail made with bourbon, sugar, mint, and crushed ice) and Vesper (a cocktail made with gin, vodka, and Lillet, which is similar to vermouth and was named after Bond girl Vesper Lynd) in the movies (Kellerman, 2015); the first cocktail ever ordered by James Bond in the 1954 version of *Casino Royale* was scotch and water (Rubin, 2021: 1611). His badass cinematic image, sexual attractiveness, and seriousness influenced his fans, and many of them mimicked his movie drinking habits.

This is an example of how celebrities promote alcoholic beverages as part of a glamorous and luxurious lifestyle. Some winemakers lure celebrities into the advertising business, just for a particular harvest or a particular wine from that harvest, and many have also entered the alcohol industry themselves as owners of their brands,[1] though their wine need not be premium by oenological criteria. Their name and shiny packaging are enough to make a good sale (Sugarfly, 2017).

[1] For example, the musician Justin Timberlake, reaper Sean "Diddy" and actor George Clooney with different types of tequila, Drew Barrymore, Angelina Jolie and Brad Pitt with champagne, David Beckham with whiskey, musician Dave Matthews with wines, reality show star Bethenny Frankel with margarita, vodka, sangria and wine, music group Hanson—MmmHop with beer, and many more (Kell, 2015; Sugarfly, 2017).

Such a strategy can also be a trap, as strategic brand management specialists like to warn. In traditional marketing, stars of stage and screen are often used in advertising. Using stars to promote luxury products is extremely dangerous. A luxury brand is courted by stars just as they are courted by journalists and paparazzi. Employing the services of a star is tantamount to saying that the brand needs some of that star's status to survive, and admitting that it has none itself. For the luxury brand, this is a gross strategic error because it turns the relationship on its head. Only brand dominance, standing over everything like a god, is acceptable, not the behavior of a mere mortal. If celebrities are used to promote the luxury product, its status is reduced to that of a mere accessory (Kapferer & Bastien, 2009: 73, 74). The use of a star is not helpful to the success of a beautiful advertising campaign, and is often even harmful, because it shields or even destroys the direct affective customer-brand relationship by replacing it with the affective customer-star relationship. In the eyes of the customer, only the dominance of the brand is legitimate, not that of an individual of any kind, certainly not that of a movie star of any kind who will go out of fashion. Often the conspicuous use of a star is a means of concealing the absence of creative ideas, in whose place comes the use of the cheque book to buy the celebrity of the moment (Kapferer & Bastien, 2009: 216).

Thus, also advertising alcohol with the help of celebrities can also be a double-edged sword, as some fall prey to addiction, like rapper T. I., who promoted Rémy Martin cognac. Others unintentionally mention certain brands, like rappers B.I.G., Bad Boy, and Jay Z, who mentioned the rather unknown Cristal champagne in their videos, which was hard to find on the market because it was a small production. In 2006, when the brand owner declared that he thought rapper Jay Z was a racist, he immediately replaced the champagne brand with Armand de Brigna, who appeared in the next video in 2009, which brought the owner a big profit as he sold all his shares several times. A similar thing happened with the Courvoisier cognac mentioned by the rapper Busta Rhymes in 2002, sales increased by 30% and the brand owner has been working with the singer ever since (Sugarfly, 2017). The unintended sales increase was also caused by Frank Sinatra praising Jack Daniels whiskey on his tour in the 1950s (Kell, 2015). Marketers also engage such celebrities who claim not to drink at all. In 2011, Midori hired Kim Kardashian, who appeared in their advertisement and tweeted, the campaign was not successful (Sugarfly, 2017). The Trump vodka advertised by Donald Trump from 2005 to 2011 was also a pure failure (Kell, 2015).

All these examples show that marketers hire celebrities because:

- They can have a strong influence on consumer purchases with their dominance in popular culture and with many followers on social networks.
- Draw attention to the new alcohol brands that use them to gain mass attention.
- Position the brand; due to their style and sophistication, they are particularly popular in the champagne industry (e.g., James Bond for Bollinger and Scarlet Johansen for Moët).
- Attract new consumers, with the alcohol industry appealing particularly to teenagers and children.

- Give fading brands a sense of excitement and desirability.
- Appeal to a particular fan base (Sugarfly, 2017).

Celebrities engaged by the alcohol industry are strategically selected, they must be credible, their advertising messages must sound authentic, they must also consume these drinks themselves, and their involvement in the alcohol campaign must not just be obvious. Their role in advertising is now largely equivalent to social media (Sugarfly, 2017).

The smart product placement technique described earlier is increasingly being used in online advertising. To increase demand for the product, well-known people (celebrities) from the fashion, music, and film industries, as well as athletes, advertise the product on social media. For example, they post photos on Facebook and Instagram that include brand logos or distinguishing shapes that allow the user to identify the manufacturer/company. The question then becomes whether such behavior can be considered legally permissible in the context of these techniques of influencing the recipient (Nowak-Gruca, 2018: 40).

Although the law generally prohibits a positive causal link between drinking alcohol and success in life, and that alcohol consumption contributes to success in social and sexual life, alcohol advertisers in some cases go against the law or violate it when attracting well-known actors to advertise alcohol or when they put beautiful girls or young people in general in alcohol ads.

Violations of advertising codes and inappropriate alcohol advertising show that alcohol traders are aware of their actions, as the most common reports (substantiated and unfounded) are from the area of discrediting their trade competitors. Unfounded reports of problematic advertising due to too frequent, inappropriate, harmful, intrusive, shameful, misleading advertising that positively affirms alcohol and alcohol consumption, is directed toward minors. They are encouraged to consume alcohol by advertising their role models. Such advertising is at the expense of the fact that advertising tribunals can decide on the compliance of advertising with the provisions of advertising codes, and not on compliance with applicable law, as they do not have the authority to do so. Besides, in some unfounded cases, advertising tribunals find that advertisers skillfully avoid violating the provisions of the Advertising Code and therefore cannot sanction them.

References

Alpen-Adria-Universität Klagenfurt/Graz/Wien. (2016, 7 July). Highly prominent product placements tend to benefit from 3D movies, while placements with low prominence lose out. *ScienceDaily*. Retrieved August 24, 2021 from www.sciencedaily.com/releases/2016/07/160707083253.htm

American Academy of Pediatrics (2017, 4 May). Alcohol marketing in popular movies doubles in past two decades: Highest increase in alcohol brand placements found in movies rated for children. *ScienceDaily*. Retrieved August 24, 2021 from www.sciencedaily.com/releases/2017/05/170504083144.htm

Heath, D. (2010). A decade of development in the anthropological study of alcohol use, 1970–1980. In *Constructive drinking. Perspectives on drink from anthropology. Mary Douglas collected works, volume X* (pp. 16–69). Routledge.

Hilliard, J. (2021a, 22 June). Alcohol in music. *Alcohol Rehab Guide*. Retrieved August 24, 2021 from https://www.alcoholrehabguide.org/alcohol/alcohol-in-popular-culture/alcohol-in-music/

Hilliard, J. (2021b, 22 June). Alcohol in TV. *Alcohol Rehab Guide*. Retrieved August 24, 2021 from https://www.alcoholrehabguide.org/alcohol/alcohol-in-popular-culture/tv/

Hoeg, N. (2021). Alcohol in popular culture: An overview. *Alcohol Rehab Guide*. April 6. Retrieved August 24, 2021 from https://www.alcoholrehabguide.org/alcohol/alcohol-in-popular-culture/

Influencers and alcohol. (2021). Eurocare. Retrieved August 24, 2021 from https://eurocare.org/cares.php?sp=commercial-communication&ssp=influencers-and-alcohol

Kapferer, J.-N., & Bastien, V. (2009). *The luxury strategy: Break the rules of marketing to build luxury brands*. Philadelphia, Kogan Page.

Kell, J. (2015, 8 January). 9 celebrities making money off your liquor shelf. *Fortune*. Retrieved August 24, 2021 from http://fortune.com/2015/01/08/celebrities-alcohol-brands/

Kellerman, A. (2015, 7 May). How James Bond Destroyed The Martini. *VinePair*. Retrieved August 24, 2021 from https://vinepair.com/wine-blog/how-james-bond-destroyed-the-martini/?utm_source=facebook&utm_content=51605&utm_campaign=pagepost&utm_medium=social&fbclid=IwAR2lZTpfIoFqwkyKPokJ8i9UUZqW8xicFDkFRmwuzcBl2JJEEm0ce5E4iFY

Morris, R. (2021 9 August). American Gen Z are thoughtful boozers, survey says. *The Drinks Business*. Retrieved August 24, 2021 from https://www.thedrinksbusiness.com/2021/08/american-gen-z-are-thoughtful-boozers-survey-says/

Muldoon, M. (2021, 22 June). Alcohol in movie. *Alcohol Rehab Guide*. Retrieved August 24, 2021 from https://www.alcoholrehabguide.org/alcohol/alcohol-in-popular-culture/movies/

Nowak-Gruca, A. (2018). Selected legal problems of online advertising. *Lexonomica, 10*(1), 33–44. Retrieved August 24, 2021 from https://journals.um.si/index.php/lexonomica/article/view/114/79

Proctor, R. N. (2011). *Golden holocaust: Origins of the cigarette catastrophe and the case for abolition*. University of California Press.

Rubin, S. J. (2021). *The James bond movie encyclopedia*. Chicago Review Press.

Sugarfly. (2017, 1 May). Are celebrity endorsements really worth the expense and headaches? *Sugarfly Innovative marketing for wine, travel and luxury brands*. Retrieved August 24 2021 from http://sugarflymarketing.com/are-celebrity-endorsements-really-worth-the-expense-and-headaches/

Chapter 14
Legislation between Norm and Practice

Take a drink because you pity yourself, and then the drink pities you and has a drink, and then two good drinks get together and that calls for drinks all around.

H. Beam Piper, Little Fuzzy

Abstract This chapter demonstrates how, despite more progressive legislation in certain countries, alcohol prohibitions and penalties are excessively lax for one of the world's most profitable industries. Because regulations and standards are not uniform, governments and regulators confront issues. The alcohol or advertising sectors frequently (co)design and manage existing legislation. The COVID-19 pandemic in 2020 and 2021 made it possible to purchase alcohol in previously prohibited ways. Because alcohol use has increased, tightening the current legally permissible alcohol advertising and adding digital media advertising in it is urgently needed.

Alcohol marketing arose as a question when youth-targeted alcopop products raised awareness at the European Union policy level. Soon afterward, preparations for the EU's first alcohol strategy (2006–2012) began (Alcohol, 2020: 11). The World Health Organization as well as many other institutions in 2020 have reaffirmed that existing legislation and codes of conduct do not match the changing nature of the advertising methods employed in the commercial sector. Social media and other online and app-based marketing techniques can reach consumers in regions where alcohol-related content is prohibited in national law (Alcohol, 2020: 3).

In the first half of the twentieth century, the first laws governing advertising activity were enacted. The American Association of Advertising Agencies (AAAA) established one of the first regulations in 1916, titled "Standards of Conduct." There are currently many legal acts in EU law that regulate the advertising market, among which we can distinguish horizontal provisions that apply to all forms of advertising and specific provisions that relate to advertising of a specific type of product or service (Nowak-Gruca, 2018: 37). In the EU, overall national regulation of visible elements of alcoholic beverage marketing and advertising includes statutory

M. Ramšak, *Social Impact of Wine Marketing*, Contributions to Management Science, https://doi.org/10.1007/978-3-030-89224-1_14

regulation, which is embodied in legislation and enacted by national governments, and non-statutory regulation, also known as self-regulation (i.e., voluntary codes of conduct, statutes, or guidelines) (Regulation, 2012: 9). Advertising and marketing regulations cover the following topics: advertising of alcoholic beverages on television, radio, the Internet, billboards, and any other publicly visible media; labeling or packaging of alcoholic beverages (regarding promotional aspects); sales promotion of alcoholic beverages; advertising of lower prices of alcoholic beverages; advertising of volume discounts of alcoholic beverages; sponsorship of events (sports, cultural, or otherwise) through alcoholic beverage advertising; sampling or interpersonal promotion of alcoholic beverages; placement and display of alcoholic beverages at points of sale; advertising via mobile phones (e.g., SMS advertising); visible sponsorship (e.g., of TV programs or events); and paid product placement (Regulation, 2012: 9). In many European countries, there is more than one alcohol marketing regulation or code.

Individual regulations in one country may differ in a variety of ways, including the type of marketing they refer to, the types of drinks they regulate, the media they regulate, and who is subject to the regulation (Regulation, 2012: 17). The majority of European countries have several regulations governing the marketing of alcoholic beverages. Only a few have only statutory regulations, and even fewer have no statutory regulation in practice: in Europe, having only a self-regulatory system is the exception. As a result, almost all European countries have chosen to legislate at least some aspects of alcohol marketing (Regulation, 2012: 29).

The ELSA project (2005–2007), which involved representatives from 24 European countries and assessed and reported on the enforcement of national laws and self-regulation in relation to the advertising and marketing of alcoholic beverages in the EU Member States and Norway, discovered several troubling features, including that the EU Recommendation not to produce alcoholic beverages in a way that appeals to children and adolescents is insufficiently covered; that the (partial) ban on or volume restriction of alcohol marketing is primarily regulated by law, and that the enforcement of marketing regulations is more frequently regulated by law than by self-regulation. It was also noted that specific temporal bans take many shapes in EU countries. They can include: They can include: a ban on alcohol advertising on the radio outside of certain hours on certain days, or a ban in cinemas or theatres before evening hours; a ban on advertising for specific types of drinks, such as a ban on spirits advertising on the radio, TV, or in cinemas between certain hours or for the entire day; a time restriction around children's programs, such as banning alcohol advertising 5 min before or after a children's program; time restrictions limiting how long alcohol advertising can be broadcast. The ELSA project also highlighted that sanctions vary in scale and form across EU countries, and that while alcohol marketing is regulated in all countries, there is significant variation in how and to what extent it is implemented (Regulation, 2012: 25, 29, 30, 31).

The Council Recommendation of 5 June 2001 on the drinking of alcohol by young people, in particular children and adolescents (2001/458/EC) states that Member States shall (1) encourage, in cooperation with the producers and the retailers of alcoholic beverages and relevant nongovernmental organizations, the establishment of effective mechanisms in the fields of promotion, marketing and retailing; (a) to ensure that producers do not produce alcoholic beverages specifically targeted at children and adolescents; (b) to ensure that alcoholic beverages are not designed or promoted to appeal to children and adolescents, with particular attention to, inter alia, the following elements: use of styles (such as characters, motifs, or colors) associated with youth culture; featuring children, adolescents, or other young-looking models in promotion campaigns; allusions to or images associated with the consumption of drugs and other harmful substances such as tobacco; links with violence or antisocial behavior; implications of social, sexual or sporting success; encouragement of children and adolescents to drink, including low-price selling to adolescents of alcoholic drinks; advertising during or sponsorship of sporting, musical or other special events in which a significant number of children and adolescents attend as actors or spectators; advertising in media targeted at children and adolescents or reaching a significant number of children and adolescents; the free distribution of alcoholic drinks to children and adolescents as well as sale or free distribution of products which are used to promote alcoholic drinks and which may appeal in particular to children and adolescents; (d) to allow manufacturers to get pre-launch advice in advance of marketing a product or investing in a product and, in the case of marketing campaigns, before they are actually launched on the market; (e) ensure that complaints against products which are not being promoted, marketed or retailed in accordance with the principles set out in points (a) and (b) can be effectively handled, and that, where appropriate, such products can be withdrawn from sale and the relevant inappropriate marketing or advertising practices stopped; (2) urge the representative producer and trade organizations of alcoholic beverages to commit themselves to comply with the principles described above (Regulation, 2012: 11).

The only EU Directive that explicitly regulates the marketing of alcoholic beverages is the Council Directive 89/552/EEC on the coordination of certain provisions laid down by law or "Television without Frontiers Directive" for short. Article 15 of the Directive states that advertising of alcoholic beverages must meet the following criteria: (a) it must not be aimed specifically at minors and, in particular, must not depict minors consuming these beverages; (b) it must not associate the consumption of alcohol with increased physical performance or driving; (c) it must not create the impression that the consumption of alcohol contributes to social or sexual success; (d) it must not claim that alcohol has therapeutic properties or that it is a stimulant, a sedative or a means of resolving personal conflicts; (e) it must not encourage excessive drinking or portray abstinence or moderation in a negative light; and (f) it must not emphasize high alcohol content as a positive characteristic of drinks (Regulation, 2012: 12).

According to the World Health Organization (Alcohol, 2020), the EU Council adopted a revision of the Audiovisual Media Services Directive in November 2018 (see: Audiovisual, 2018). The revision included elements such as a strengthened Country of Origin Principle, rule extensions to cover video-sharing platforms, improved minor protection, and strengthened provisions to protect children from inappropriate audiovisual commercial communications for foods high in saturated fat, salt, and/or free sugars. In terms of alcohol, the revised version made no significant changes to its predecessor. The Audiovisual Media Services Directive does not specifically apply to alcohol advertising and has been criticized for being content-oriented rather than frequency-focused. It has been chastised by the European Public Health Alliance for failing to protect children, empower parents, or encourage governments to act forcefully (see: AVMSD, 2017). Public health advocates have pointed out that the European counter-lobby is too powerful to allow stronger directives, and that governments must work for stricter national regulations. However, it should be noted that the Audiovisual Media Services Directive is a minimum harmonization directive, which means that European Union member states are free to implement more comprehensive provisions on their respective territories (Alcohol, 2020: 3). To protect the youngest and most vulnerable segments of the population, most European countries have implemented policies regulating alcohol advertising. The regulatory policies put in place range from outright bans with legal penalties to industry-adopted self-regulatory codes of conduct. It is asserted that the self-regulatory codes of conduct adopted by the alcohol and marketing industries provide an effective means of monitoring good marketing standards. Several scientific reviews, however, have questioned the effectiveness of such codes, pointing out that the rules are frequently violated and vaguely formulated, creating loopholes and room for ambiguous content. 15 of the 53 WHO European Region Member States (28%) have a total statutory ban on all alcohol marketing (beer, wine, and spirits) across television, radio, print media, and point of sale; 22 Member States (42%) have only partial statutory restrictions; and 16 (30%) have only a voluntary agreement, self-regulation, or no regulations at all. The most stringent policies apply to spirit commercials, which are prohibited on national television in 43 percent ($n = 23$) of all countries. Wine advertising bans are slightly less common; for example, 30 percent ($n = 16$) of countries prohibit wine commercials on national television. Beer commercial bans appear to be even rarer—for example, 19% (10 countries) prohibit beer commercials in print media, while 25% (13 countries) prohibit them on national television (Alcohol, 2020: 5–6).

Alcohol marketers must follow not only national legislation and self-regulatory rules established by the alcohol industry when using social media platforms, but also policies established by social media companies (Alcohol, 2020: 11). In 2018, Facebook and Instagram mandated that all alcohol advertisements adhere to national legislation and industry standards. Pages that promote the sale of alcoholic beverages and other regulated goods must restrict access to users aged 18 years and above, and when national law requires it, age verification should be set higher. For example, alcohol advertisements aimed at a Swedish audience must be directed at people aged 25 years and above. Twitter had stipulations about alcohol advertising on its platform the same year—for example, it prohibits advertising of alcoholic beverages and related items to minors. There are also some country-specific rules: for example, online sales and branding advertisements for alcoholic beverages with an alcohol content greater than 22% are not permitted in posts aimed at Finnish audiences. Alcohol branding and promotion are permitted on YouTube, but according to 2018

YouTube guidelines, alcohol advertisements must be in accordance with laws and industry standards, and never target individuals under the legal drinking age. The restrictions also apply to the promotion of nonalcoholic beverages that resemble alcoholic beverages, such as beer, wine, or cocktails (Alcohol, 2020: 11).

Alcohol marketing regulation is a matter of political will. While many European countries still have only non-statutory alcohol marketing regulations in place, new digital marketing is posing new challenges for public health policies. Globally synergized, interactive, and multimodal campaigns with content ranging from games to YouTuber branding, competitions, quizzes, and video clips are difficult to discern and monitor, and they are difficult to translate into objects of effective legislation and oversight. The issue of limiting content on social media is largely defined by how we define advertising in online environments. New native advertising techniques can be difficult to detect for both children and adults. It can be difficult to determine the commercial interests and senders behind messages at times. Because almost everything an alcoholic beverage brand posts on social media helps to build the brand and raise brand awareness, separating advertising from editorial messages has also proven to be a difficult task. Some aspects of regulation can still be translated from older media principles, such as content restriction and age limits, which can still be enforced online. However, much of what is published cannot be neatly compartmentalized in traditional advertising terms. If a country decides to limit certain aspects of posts, resources must be set aside for the development of control tools, supervision, and enforcement. Effective penalty systems, such as shutting down web pages and blocking content and social media profiles, should be part of proper enforcement. However, a more straightforward and cost-effective policy option would be to outright prohibit the presence of alcohol producers in social media environments. If a total ban is not possible, partial statutory restrictions on the content of online posts should be implemented. In this case, adequate resources should be set aside for active supervision and strict policy enforcement. Because thousands of posts are published on a variety of platforms every day, this is a time-consuming but critical task. A protocol to help distinguish native advertising, user-generated content, and other commercial messages that may be difficult to understand or interpret is urgently needed. Consumers, particularly young consumers and children, are likely to be unaware of the true senders of such material. Given that many young people use social media as a natural part of their daily lives, the very least a jurisdiction should do is demand that alcohol brands properly enforce age verification. Implementing age restrictions on (for example) Facebook and Instagram pages is a simple and straightforward process. This is the bare minimum that should be expected to protect children and teenagers and prevent underage users from accessing alcohol-related posts. Member States should take a consistent stance on marketers' legal obligation to accurately tag media content and prevent inappropriate content from reaching children (Alcohol, 2020: 13–14).

In 2020 and 2021, at the time of the COVID-19 pandemic, one of the biggest changes in consumer behavior occurred as it became easier for consumers to purchase alcohol online, and as more consumers used e-commerce platforms, the alcohol industry faced challenges in the absence of adequate regulation. As e-commerce of alcohol gained momentum globally, lawmakers had to catch up by amending legislation. The rise of e-commerce, combined with COVID-19, has resulted in the liberalization of alcohol policies, for example, e-commerce markets have been quick to offer improved online purchasing solutions for consumers, bars and restaurants were allowed to sell alcohol to go while a number of more traditional markets that had previously banned alcohol e-commerce have begun to change their regulations.

References

Alcohol.org. (2020). *Drinking alcohol when working from home*. Retrieved August 24, 2021 from https://www.alcohol.org/guides/work-from-home-drinking/

Audiovisual Media Services Directive (AVMSD). (2018). Brussels: European Commission. Retrieved August 24, 2021 from https://ec.europa.eu/digital-single-market/en/audiovisual-media-services-directive-avmsd

AVMSD vote fails to ensure a healthier, future-proof marketing environment. (2017). Brussels: European public health alliance. Retrieved August 24, 2021 from https://epha.org/avmsd-vote-fails-to-ensure-a-healthier-future-proof-marketing-environment

Nowak-Gruca, A. (2018). Selected legal problems of online advertising. *Lexonomica, 10*(1), 33–44. Retrieved August 24, 2021 from https://journals.um.si/index.php/lexonomica/article/view/114/79

Regulation (EU) No 1151/2012 of European Parliament and of the Council of 21 November 2012 on quality schemes for agricultural products and foodstuffs; Consolidated version (OJ L 343, 14. 12. 2012, p. 1) Retrieved August 24, 2021 from https://eur-lex.europa.eu/eli/reg/2012/1151/2019-12-14

Chapter 15
Conclusion: The Unplugged Path to Alcoholism

Alcohol won't solve your problems.

Abstract The basic purpose of the alcohol industry—to increase alcohol sales—is presented in anthropologically colored chapters that analyze some of the most severe concerns about wine and alcohol marketing today. The focus is on the wine industry, which employs modern technologies to contact potential drinkers and, via carefully planned marketing techniques, outruns alcohol legislation and preventive and curative health care for alcoholics and those on the verge of becoming alcoholics.

The book *Social Impact of Wine Marketing – The Challenge of Digital Technologies to Regulation* examines some of the most pressing concerns surrounding the societal impact of wine and alcohol marketing today. Its chapters describe how the alcohol industry, particularly the wine industry, uses modern technology to reach potential customers. The anthropological lens is used to explain marketing methods that use new technology or a 360-degree strategy to reach customers through the media landscape, as well as why legislation, self-regulation, and public health are so powerless in practice. The global situation in terms of the societal consequences of alcohol consumption is highlighted in fourteen chapters, aided by the savvy use of new technology and the alcohol industry's understanding of why people drink.

The alcohol industry's marketing efforts are incredibly effective, and they employ a variety of guerrilla tactics that are not covered by the law. Even the most receptive young generations, who are still forming their identities and worldviews, are susceptible to the industry. The alcohol sector has a significant strategic advantage in that it has excellent awareness of the primary shopping levers of the younger generation, which responds to first impressions and referrals from friends and is competent in the use of new technology. The goal of the alcohol industry that has a huge budget is clear: to increase alcohol sales. Its communication channels are aimed at individuals of all generations, but they understand young people's buying habits

M. Ramšak, *Social Impact of Wine Marketing*, Contributions to Management Science, https://doi.org/10.1007/978-3-030-89224-1_15

and how to cater to them with relevant mobile, multisensory methods as well as traditional communication.

For the time being, however, public health has neither the staff nor the resources to keep up with these marketing strategies, let alone overtake them with effective prevention. However, the reason why anti-alcohol campaigns are not as successful as those who advertise alcohol is not only a lack of political preparedness, which is reflected in modest resources for them—after all, the state budgets are also linked to harmful habits of citizens (e.g., cigarette tax and alcohol tax) but also in the fact that these campaigns are mostly not likeable. Anti-alcohol campaigns are too long, boring and depressing, and some are just miserable because they have not yet won that positive images sell better than negative ones. They do not use even minimal techniques of emotional addressing. They work on the principle of informational intimidation, while alcohol marketing tries to please, entertain, and relax, knowing that in such a mood many protective mechanisms will collapse.

It may sound paradoxical, but anti-alcohol campaigns will have to learn a lot from the masters of alcohol marketing if they are to achieve their goal. However, I am afraid that the school years have long been missed and that the remediation of the damage can only take place in the form of a cure.

With such an expansion of global alcohol e-marketing, legal warnings sound rather anachronistic (e.g., that alcohol consumption and excessive drinking can be harmful to health, that it is forbidden to advertise alcohol in certain media, in certain places and times, that it is forbidden to sell alcohol to minors, that the sale of alcohol at certain hours is prohibited, that alcohol is prohibited for young drivers). The use of new information technologies and robotics has changed economic trends and consumer habits in such a way that the legal system has not been able to follow these changes. For the alcohol industry, the Internet is a real paradise, as drinkers can order alcohol from home, get it at home, checking the age of the customer is awkward, so alcohol can be obtained by any minor. Besides, calls from public health workers and publications for responsible alcohol dispensing do not have the right effect, as bars in the vicinity of high schools, serve alcohol to students without hindrance, being aware that inspections are rare and penalties are low. When there is an acute shortage of service staff (because they are underpaid), waiters cannot even be quickly instructed on responsible alcohol service, the main aim of which is to reduce excessive drinking, intoxication and alcohol poisoning, and to prevent minors and other vulnerable groups from drinking alcohol. Nor do they explain to untrained bartenders the significant legal restrictions on serving to minors or intoxicated persons, the time and place restrictions on serving alcohol, alternative nonalcoholic beverages of the same or a lower price range, the rules for serving at sporting events, and the like. To make matters even more absurd, student services that offer work to students occasionally offer work in bars, which includes "guiding foreigners through nightclubs and bars in the city." In the jargon of drinkers' expectations, it is simply a matter that "everyone gets drunk," but the consequences of such local drinking excursions for the alcohol industry are no longer interesting. So, on the one hand, we have restrictions and the creation of a kind of anti-alcohol quarantine for young people, and on the other hand, unrestricted access to alcohol on all sides. Those who are supposed to get alcohol as little as possible can even serve it.

In advertising practice, we observe many subtle noncompliance with legal provisions, which are most often reflected in the insufficient size of the letters of the advertising message, which, regardless of the medium, must contain a warning text that alcohol consumption might be harmful to health. This warning is often not well visible from the background of the advertisements and is not legible and, despite the ban, emphasizes the invigorating or calming effects of alcohol, which suggest that alcohol consumption solves personality problems, leads to a better, happier and more successful life, better social and sexual life, or greater physical capacity and the like.

There is an urgent need to modernize and tighten the current legally permitted alcohol advertising and to include digital media advertising in it. The implementation of existing legislation needs to be optimized; industry practices in the field of digital advertising and the self-regulation of the alcohol industry should be monitored; the impact of social media and media marketing on alcohol consumption and health consequences needs to be assessed.

Index

M. Ramšak, *Social Impact of Wine Marketing*, Contributions to Management Science, https://doi.org/10.1007/978-3-030-89224-1

T

The manufacturer's authorised representative in the EU is Springer Nature Customer Service Centre GmbH, Europaplatz 3, 69115 Heidelberg, Germany. If you have any concerns regarding our products, please contact ProductSafety@springernature.com

Printed and bound by CPI Group (UK) Ltd, Croydon, CR0 4YY
30/09/2026
02225608-0009